How to Shoot
a Feature Film
for Under
$10,000

*AND NOT GO TO JAIL

How to Shoot a Feature Film

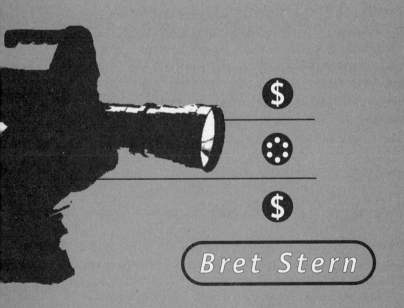

$

⊙

$

Bret Stern

for Under $10,000 *

*AND NOT GO TO JAIL

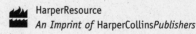
HarperResource
An Imprint of HarperCollins*Publishers*

This book was previously published by Raintree County Press in April 1999 (ISBN 1-892877-00-7).

HarperCollins books may be purchased for educational, business, or sales promotional use. For information please write: Special Markets Department, HarperCollins Publishers Inc., 10 East 53rd Street, New York, New York 10022.

Designed by Judith Stagnitto Abbate / Abbate Design

LIBRARY OF CONGRESS CATALOGING-IN-PUBLICATION DATA

Stern, Bret.
    How to shoot a feature film for under $10,000 : and not go to jail / by Bret Stern.
      p. cm.
    Originally published: New York : Raintree County Press, 2000.
    ISBN 0-06-008467-7 (alk. paper)
    1. Motion pictures—Production and direction. 2. Low budget motion pictures. I. Title.
PN1995.9.P7S717 2002
791.43'0232—dc21

                                2002022993

04 05 06 WB/RRD 10 9 8 7 6 5

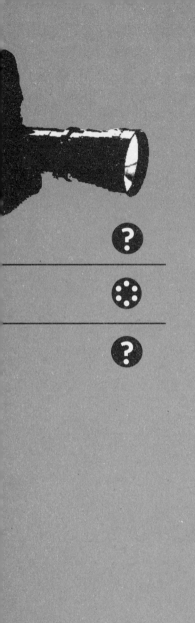

Contents

Chapter 3 What Does It Take to Make
a Feature Film? ——————(38)

Chapter 6   Preparing to Shoot ————— (115)

Chapter 7   The Shoot — (131)

Chapter 8 Digital Video — 152

Chapter 11 Sound ——————————————— 212

Chapter 12   Film Festivals ─────────── (225)

Rules to Live By in Order to Retain One's Sanity While Trying to Break Into the Film Business — (274)

Disclaimer

The author of this book in no way recommends breaking any law. He is not a lawyer, and while he would like to give you advice on how to bend the law, that would be far out of his jurisdiction as a filmmaker. The illegal schemes and tactics described in this book are hyperbole used by the author for comedic effect. If you don't know what hyperbole is, look it up in the dictionary. Mr. Stern, that means you too. But to make a long story short . . . don't get him in trouble.

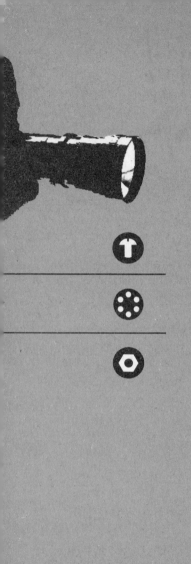

Foreword

*i*f you're reading this introduction while still in the bookstore and you're considering buying this book, let me first ask you a question: Ever thought of going into the kitchen-remodeling business?

Remodeling your kitchen is perhaps the single most efficient way to increase the equity in your house (or your parents' house). Buy a $4 kitchen-remodeling magazine, go to Home Depot and buy $10,000 worth of faux-granite linoleum and track lighting (on your girlfriend's credit card), and spend a few weeks remodeling the kitchen (Home Depot's great about teaching you how to install all this stuff). Once it looks good, go to your bank and ask for a home equity loan. They'll send an appraiser who will spend ten minutes walking through your house. He'll be very impressed with the kitchen and instantly appraise your house for at least $10,000 more than it's worth. Get that home equity loan for $20,000, pay off your girlfriend's credit card and now you have $10,000 to make a film if you still really want to. And if all else fails, you can go into the kitchen-remodeling business full-time.

If the aforementioned means of living your life appeals to

your sense of stealth, gumption, and pluck, then perhaps you are cut out to be a filmmaker. One more test, though: Go back to Home Depot and, still using your girlfriend's credit card, buy two sheets of two-by-three-foot Peg-Board and a short length of speaker wire. You're now ready to make a sandwich board. Write something on it. Anything. Protesting whales, advocating the end of the world, or just claiming to be a disabled Vietnam vet asking for money. Now stand on a street corner for a day and humiliate yourself. Better yet, take your pants off first and then do this. Don't worry—sticking to the title of this book, you can't go to jail for wearing a sandwich board even if that's the only thing you're wearing: It's not indecent exposure as long as the board covers your bits and pieces, and it's not unauthorized advertising (even on private property) if you can claim that it's clothing and not a sign.

By the end of the day your back will hurt, you will have bloody gashes in your shoulders, and several people will have spit on you. Still want to make a movie? *Now* you're ready to start reading this book.

Filmmaking, as you'll learn in these pages, has almost nothing to do with art, talent, or even family connections. It has largely to do with humiliation, and the ability to withstand the worst forms of indignity for extended periods of time. If you're one of those people who religiously collected your rejection letters from all those Ivy League schools you didn't get into, you might be cut out to make a film. If you're one of those people who then scanned those Ivy League letterheads, printed out your own stationery, and sent forged acceptance letters to the Department of Education in order to secure student loans and grants, then you're definitely cut out to be a filmmaker (and now you can afford to be—without having to set one foot in Home Depot)!

This book is a very clear and concise step-by-step guide to making and promoting an independent film. I've known Bret Stern for years, and if there's one person who can teach the fine art of resourceful filmmaking, it's Bret. I think I first encountered him when he submitted his film *Road to Park City* to the Slamdance Film Festival, of which I'm one of the founders (when you read the ChapStick story, that's me he's talking about).

A lot of people make the ill-fated choice of making a film about making a film. What they fail to realize is just how many other people are making films about how to make films. Further, they fail to realize just how many festival programmers, distribution executives, and film critics really hate to see films about making films. But Bret's film was different. For one thing, it was good. The script was clever, the style was unique, the acting was good, and the editing was sharp. That's the key—the editing. Filmmakers often make the mistake of spending way too much time and money trying to make their films look good and give them "production value." (For those who haven't read the book yet, that means fancy lights, a pricey camera, and a cinematographer who just wants to have sex with your lead actress.) But for the kind of money you have to make your film, you'll never be able to compete with Hollywood films, so don't try.

Your biggest luxury is time, so you should put it to good use: the script, rehearsals, editing, and sound. (Remember, the difference between good production sound and bad is more about finding a quiet location and waiting for the planes to clear than it is about renting an expensive microphone.) And it doesn't matter how clever your script is if you can't hear it. Who cares if your film is grainy and out of focus—just tell people that's intentional and artistic. Look, *Clerks* was a fantastically successful $27,000 film that looked like it was shot for $10,000. Christopher Nolan made his first film, *Following*, for under ten grand, and that was in England—where it's a lot harder to find free equipment, competitive labs, and cheap labor (or "labour," as the case may be).

Now keep in mind, you're not reading a book by Kevin Smith or Christopher Nolan. These guys are now both very successful studio-level writer-directors who also have young kids at home with diapers to change. Neither of them has the time to write a book these days. And besides, would you rather learn about the one-tenth of 1 percent of independent filmmakers who lucked out, or the real story of how 99.9% of indie filmmakers actually get their movies made? That's where Bret comes in. He made a great film that unfortunately was not a commercial success. In other words, he knows what he's talking about. He's suffered indignities from beginning to end and isn't too distracted by either a successful filmmaking career or a perfect family life to write a book. Nope, Bret's had plenty of time on his hands to craft a carefully researched, insightful tome on how *most* of us actually make our films (and occasionally stay out of jail).

And Bret will also teach you another valuable lesson: Always talk about yourself. He doesn't waste a lot of time giving examples from other people's films. Why give them free press when you can get it yourself? This book is being published by Harper-Collins—one of the biggest publishers out there. Several people (OK, a few people) are going to read this book, and maybe one of them will be an investor who wants to give Bret some money to make another film. More important, maybe one of them will want to give me money so I can make another commercially unsuccessful film. See what I did there? I changed the subject to start talking about me. That's an important rule of filmmaking. Always talk about yourself, or better yet, always talk about me. Did I mention my film *Omaha (the movie)* just came out on DVD and you can buy it from my Web site at www.slamdance.com/mirvish? See how easy that is?

Go ahead and keep reading this book. If you liked the foreword, I can assure you that the rest of the book is longer. (Editor's note: And way better!) So sit back and enjoy. As for me, I've got a kitchen to go remodel.

Filmmaker Dan Mirvish cofounded the Slamdance Film Festival when his film Omaha (the Movie) *got rejected from Sundance. The film* went on to play in over thirty international film festivals, and when no distributor picked it up, Mirvish strapped on a sandwich board and self-distributed the film to over thirty-five U.S. cities. To find out how you can help him make his next film, check out www.slam-dance.com/mirvish.

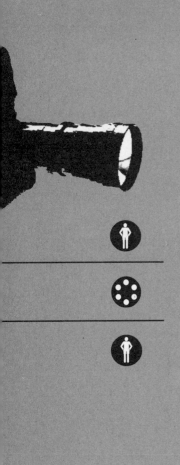

The Author Would Like to Say . . .

This book is for all those who have ever attempted to make their filmmaking dream a reality. For those who sacrifice their gastrointestinal systems and are willing to forgo a hutch and china set in order to buy that extra roll of film. These are the people who really know what being a filmmaker is all about, and they deserve a little recognition. I'd like to thank John Viener, to whom I promised a Red Lobster commercial (and no, John, you can't send me an invoice because your name is in print); Karl Kempter, the only person I can spend five straight hours with talking about nothing but *Das Boot*—the director's cut, of course: anybody who has ever crewed on one of my films, especially those who had to sleep on cots in a bar in Wallingford, Connecticut, for a week and take showers with a hose in the basement—and most especially Steve, who has gotten caught up in many of my feature filmmaking schemes; and Eric Wright, who was the first to see what this book really could be and did something about it. Of course, I wouldn't want to forget my good friend Peter, and my agent (yes, I like saying that) Paula, and Edwin, my editor, whose gentle prodding produced a better book, and, of course, Barbara the Whoobies.

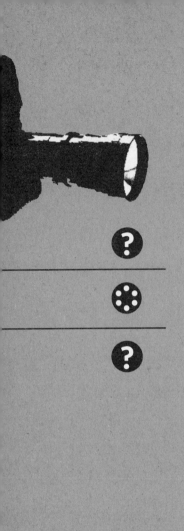

Let's make a movie

chapter

ow can I make a feature film? Man has been asking this question since the dawn of time (or at least since the invention of the motion-picture camera and projector). The answer: Just start making your feature-length film, and eventually it will get finished. Get the wheels in motion. First convince yourself that you are making a motion picture. Then convince others of the same. Before you know it, you will have a completed film—and, quite possibly, an eviction notice.

The only thing standing between you and your completed feature-length motion picture is money. It's that simple. Everything you need to make your film has a price tag, and more often than not a grossly exaggerated one that has no basis in reality.

So I pose this question: What are you going to do about it?

Are you going to sit back and complain that there is no possible way you can afford to shoot your feature film, or are you going to dive in headfirst and start making your celluloid dream a reality? If you are ready to commit to making a feature film for a bargain-basement price while avoiding the penal system and all it has to offer, then read on.

How to Begin

The first step in low-budget filmmaking is to identify your financial situation. So let's take a look at what types of funds you may have available and the implications that will have upon you as a filmmaker.

 NO-BUDGET *filmmaker.* You have no money. You own nothing. You travel by public transit. Your credit cards are almost maxed out and your girlfriend pays the rent. Your latest harebrained scheme is to direct a feature-length film. This type of filmmaker is in the most peril of going to jail.

 LOW-BUDGET *filmmaker.* You have saved up a little money and, for the most part, are free of debt. Your car seems to run OK, so you are ready to make the plunge into feature filmmaking.

 ASSHOLE *filmmaker.* You have a wallet full of platinum and gold cards. You drive a new car; it's a BMW or a Lexus. You are not really worried about money. You have several trust funds and a large inheritance in your future. You make movies for fun and to meet attractive members of the opposite or same sex.

The no-budget and low-budget filmmakers are basically in the same boat. In the world of filmmaking, there is almost no difference between being broke and having a few thousand dollars saved up, although having a semireliable car definitely gives the low-budget filmmaker a slight edge. If you are one of these first two types, you will have to learn to think around money. Thinking up ingenious solutions to costly problems will become your hobby, and a necessary one. You will learn to use your financial straits to your advantage. In short, you will become a penny-pinching filmmaking machine.

The asshole filmmakers have a whole different set of problems to expect. At least, problems when it comes to making films. For instance, say you have a lot of money. You might be tempted to go out and get the best of everything: the best camera, the best lights, and the best crew. All this will cost you a large portion of your trust fund, but you figure it's worth it because, with the best of everything, how can your film fail? All this might be in vain. You run the real risk of losing your story in the logistical empire you have assembled. As a first-time director, you can easily be overwhelmed by the needs of your cast and crew. It's a classic adage: The stupider you are, the more money you are going to need. And conversely, the more money you have, the stupider you will become. To avoid this—be smart, spend wisely.

One thing, however, is common to all filmmakers: the inevitability of suffering from crippling self-doubt, nervous breakdowns, and/or heart failure.

Now that you know what type of filmmaker you are, let's level the playing field. For the purposes of this book, we are on a mission to complete a feature-length motion picture for $10,000 or less. With this tight budget, throwing money at a problem is not going to be allowed. No, we are going to be faster, stronger, and better than the next filmmaker. Prepare yourself to become the Six Million Dollar Man of feature film production—if *The Six Million Dollar Man* had been made for ten grand or less.

Types of Filmmaking

There are many types of films coming out of Hollywood today. The type of film we are all most familiar with is called the studio **A picture.** The A in A picture means that the people involved with the films are from the A list of actors, directors, and so on. Just like

Hollywood itself, the A list does not really exist. It is a perception created by word of mouth, marketing, public relations (PR), and the finanacial performance of their most recent motion pictures.

The average studio A picture has a big star attached and lots of money behind it. The actual shooting of the film will take approximately twelve weeks. From start to finish, the film takes about a year to complete and can cost anywhere from $30 million to $300 million. It will be released to thousands of screens simultaneously in the hopes of having a record first weekend. The goal of this is to break the $200 million gross mark and become the next blockbuster hit. In order to have a strong opening, a lot of money will be spent on advertising and promotion before the film opens in theaters. After a film's opening week, it will usually live or die based on word of mouth. No amount of advertising can overcome the word of mouth a motion picture generates, good or bad.

The average **B film** has lots of action, an up-and-coming star (or a has-been star) in the lead, and costs anywhere from $2 million to $20 million. The films can be easily recognized by their cast. These films are usually released around the blockbusters with the hope of becoming a sleeper hit.

The third type of film is the **independent** (or **indie**) **film**. These films usually have a budget anywhere from $10,000 to $500,000 and are often shot on 16-mm film or some type of video format. The goal of these films is to gain acceptance into a film festival. From there, the producer hopes to gain enough recognition to have the film picked up by a major distributor and then released theatrically, either in the United States or abroad. At the very least, the hope is to get either a video or a cable distribution deal. The director of the film hopes to garner good reviews and industry buzz so he or she can get financing for a new film and possibly have their entrée to the A list.

That brings us to the arty stuff. These films are instantly recognizable. They can be either period pieces with the cast talking in cockney or the fringe picture that delves into the seedier side of anything the filmmaker chooses to examine. They often have very weak stories and great reviews. These films seem to emanate from Europe and tend to be made by people with the titles Lord and Sir followed by a bunch of middle names.

This is what you are up against, but it is nothing a little American ingenuity can't solve. Yes, you are going to do better, faster, and for less . . . or die trying.

What Kind of Film Am I Making?

Now that you have committed to becoming a filmmaker, you need to ask, "What kind of film will I be making?" At this point in your filmmaking career, you are an unknown speck in the filmmaking cosmos. You cannot afford to make an arty-preachy film that expresses your views on everything from world politics to the virtues of irradiating food. Nor can you tell the heart-wrenching story of the long-distance runner. No way. Your film has two purposes: First, to get you noticed by the big guys in Hollywood. Second, to make you independently wealthy.

To succeed, you will need a great script and a fresh approach to attract the attention of the powers that may be. While making some money would be nice, the real goal of your independent film should be to get your second film financed by somebody who does not share your surname. Now, we have all heard people mutter the phrase "independent film," but what exactly does this term mean, anyway? Basically, the driving force behind any film is money. The equation is simple: no money = no film. When a studio finances a film, they own it. By owning it, they control it. On the other hand, an independent film is controlled by some entity independent of a studio. Notice that I did not say the director is in control of the film. That's right. Independent films can be made by anyone, including corporations, groups of dentists, or a young director who has just convinced his parents to take out a second mortgage on their house. The essential truth is that money talks, and if it's your money you can do whatever you want.

The outlet for delivery of your independent film is the ever-growing network of film festivals in America and throughout the world. The film festivals are the independent filmmakers' equivalent of the sneak preview that studios conduct for all their films. If a preview does poorly, a studio may shelve a film. If you don't get into any festivals, you might be forced to do the same. If a Hollywood film does marvelously in a preview, a studio will get excited about it and throw resources behind it. If your film generates great reviews and incredible word of mouth, then a studio might get behind it—meaning they will buy it from you. It's all the same game, just different tracks and verbiage.

If you want to make your money back, then make an exploitation movie.* This genre stands a good chance of getting distributed in the home video market and perhaps the much coveted 1 A.M. screening slot on either Showtime or Cinemax, not to mention the television sales to Guam and upper Manitoba. If you are a truly gifted person, or just a good talker, you can look forward to a slim to almost nonexistent chance of a theatrical distribution. After your distributor has sold off these markets and you have completed the first round of lawsuits that may be necessary to collect your money from the film's distributor, you might then have earned enough to pay back the production costs of the film. Those are the odds: take 'em or leave 'em.

Getting Noticed

Here's one piece of advice no matter what kind of film you make: Be controversial. You want as much buzz as you can get, and mak-

*Not a legally binding promise.

ing a film that upsets people is a sure way to get interest. We all want articles in *Variety,* the *Hollywood Reporter,* and all the other film trade papers.

Even if your film is not controversial, you can still promote it by being different. Think up quirky stories about your life and why you have become a filmmaker; perhaps your parents locked you in a closet with a super-8 camera for a week. Think *way* out. The crazier your stories are, the better. Exploit yourself and, if necessary, lie. If a reporter asks you a question like "How do you feel society will gain from your film?" you might respond with "I'm glad you asked. I recently sold a kidney to raise money for this film, and Abe Lincoln visits me often in my kitchen." This answer doesn't match the question, but it makes you sound committed to your project and a bit eccentric. If you are desperate for press, tell a story about having sex with a famous celebrity.

What's Your Idea?

All filmmaking starts with an idea. Chances are you picked up this book because you have an idea and don't know quite how to proceed. Well, what is your idea?

Think for a moment. Relax. Get a good picture of it in your mind.

Got it? Good.

Yeah, you like it, don't you?

Well, here's a news flash—you can't do it. It's a terrible idea. You can't afford it. It's boring and plotless and nobody cares. Your idea sucks and you suck. Give up!

Now, take a breath. Go splash some water on your face. I'll wait.

Good, you're back. You have just been reborn (and you

thought it only worked in the movies). Now, I'm going to ask you again. What is your idea?

If you stick to your original idea, then you have what it takes to be a filmmaker. Over the coming months, you will constantly face doubters and detractors, and you need to learn now to be your own best friend and believer. Others of you will be second-guessing yourselves, your confidence shaken. You will begin jumping from one idea to another. That is where the trouble begins. Until you truly believe in your idea, you will not succeed. To write a script, you must focus on a single idea. You must live, breathe, and eat it. It must consume you. So, before you start writing a script, settle on one idea and stick to it; a drawer full of half-finished scripts is not going to help anyone.

Now, it's time to write the script. Sound intimidating? Yeah. Are you ready to work? No, don't say you'll do it tomorrow. Cancel your plans to go sunbathing, forget about lunch at Taco Bell with your best buddy—you are going to write *today*.

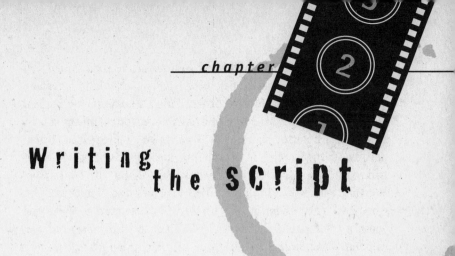

Writing the script

How to Start

The chances of making a good film without a script are about the same as winning Powerball; for those who bought a ticket this week, the odds are exactly 80 million to 1. The good news is that the script is one of the easiest and cheapest aspects of making your film. For starters, you don't have to rely on anybody or anything. All you need is a pencil, some paper, and a fully stocked bar. For those of you who are on the wagon, iced tea is a decent substitute for those dark, manly drinks you will be inhaling to get into the proper frame of mind as a writer. You also might want to look into getting a personal computer. After all, this is the twenty-first century. Those of you who insist on writing freehand, listen up. Nobody wants to read your chicken scratch, and eventually it's going to have to be typed anyhow, so save yourself the time and expense—work on a computer! However, no checking your e-mail.

Now, you can't just write any script. No, this little gem has to be tailor-made for your needs as a low-budget filmmaker. As you write the screenplay, keep in mind your ability to successfully film what you write. You may envision the lead character being involved in a ten-car smashup on Main Street during a homecoming parade, but your wallet screams out for two bicycles colliding on the barren streets of a deserted small town. How do you decide? Well, if you have two bikes hanging in your garage that you might be willing to part with, that makes the choice fairly easy, doesn't it?

But, you're thinking, that's limiting the creative process. Not true. This is amplifying it. You need to be more creative. And since you are just beginning the script, you can craft a story that you can actually shoot.

Make a list of resources that are available to you. If your uncle has a boat, then consider writing a scene that takes place on a boat. You might have an old car that you were going to donate to the L'Chaim Charity. Instead, why not keep it and blow it up in your film? Eventually, you will work your way through this balancing act and will have a completed script for a low-budget feature film. The trick is to keep faithful to your story as you negotiate the necessities of low-budget filmmaking.

The script is your blueprint. You are the architect, which means that you have to work within certain formal conventions of writing. Namely, your script needs to be in the right format.

What Is Script Format?

First, adjust your left margin on your typewriter or word processor to about 17 so you don't lose any of your description when you bind the pages together. Next, set a tab at about 35. This is where you place the characters' names, in caps, for dialogue. Next, place another tab at 25. This is where you will start the characters' dialogue. End it at about 55 so it occupies a neat little column in the center of the page. Single-space everything, and skip a line between descriptive paragraphs and the character speaking. Page numbers go on the upper right corner and start numbering on page 2. That's about it. Better yet, buy—no, borrow—one of those nifty scriptwriting software programs.

Here is a sample scene in proper script format. This scene is an excerpt taken from the Slamdance 2000 Competition film *Road to Park City*, a low-budget film about a first-time director trying to make a film.

```
---------------------------------
INT. APARTMENT — DAY


JOHN, mid 20s, handsome, enters apartment. He holds
a bottle of champagne. He approaches TRACY, mid 20s,
smart but sexy, who is busy with some red sauce in the
kitchen.


                    JOHN
          I'm going to make a film.


                    TRACY
          That's nice.


                    JOHN
          I'm going to take it to Sundance
          and win.


                    TRACY
          Great, could you pass me the salt.


                    JOHN
          I quit my job.
```

                    TRACY
                   (angry)
          Are you out of your fuckin' mind?

                    JOHN
          No, I'm going to need all my time
          to create my film.

                    TRACY
          Create? What do you know about
          creating film?

                    JOHN
          How hard can it be? Everybody
          seems to be making one these days.

Tracy moves closer to John, she takes his hand into hers.

                    TRACY
          Yes, but these people know what
          they're doing, you don't have any
          idea how to make a film. John,
          listen to me, you're going to need
          actors, a DP, AC, gaffer, grip,
          soundman, a couple of PA's, and
          the goddamn best boy.

                    JOHN
          I've got friends.

                    TRACY
          Sure, but do they have Panavision
          cameras and HMI lighting? I don't
          think so.

John reaches for a pad and starts to scribble things down as she says them.

                    TRACY
          You're going to need to rent that
          stuff, and before they rent it to you
          they're going to want insurance,
                    (breaking down)
          and we don't even have dental.
                    (catching herself)
          All that stuff is going to cost
          money, John, lots of money.

Tracy looks around, thinking.

                    TRACY
          I can't go through this again,
          John.

Tracy starts to back away from John. She moves out into the hallway. John follows.

                    JOHN
          Wait, you're leaving me?

                    TRACY
          You're giving me no choice.

She brushes past him. Opens the door. Looks back. Pauses. Closes it. John is alone.

Notice how much space is on the page. Script format is a way to stretch twenty-five single-spaced pages into a hundred or so script-formatted pages. First, take a look at the descriptions or

action areas. These are the parts of the script that are not dialogue.

> She brushes past him. Opens the door. Looks back.
> Pauses. Closes it. John is alone.

The descriptions should be short and concise. You want the
reader to quickly grasp your ideas. Let's talk visuals; this is the
best way to build a strong script. You want the reader to envision
your characters in the world you have created, and there is no better way than with adjectives. Use lots of juicy adjectives. And
don't worry about grammatical perfection or proper usage of
words. As long as the reader can easily follow your story there are
no grammatical rules. Just spell correctly!

Also, the first time you introduce a character in the action
line, his or her name will be in CAPITALS. And if the reader needs
to be aware of a specific sound, that, too, must be in all CAPITALS.

You need to use the abbreviations EXT. (exterior) and INT.
(interior) at the beginning of every scene, followed by the location
and the time of day.

That's pretty much all you need to know.

However, besides format, there is another reason I chose the
previous scene. The text may sound familiar to you, as if it were
taken from a real situation in the life of a real first-time director.
That is a big part of screenwriting. Take what you know and put it
into a scene. When you are close to your material, the audience
will sense this and take more interest. Also, writing about what
you know and what surrounds you keeps the budget down.

So What Kind of Film Am I Going to Make?

Today, there are two types of films that can be made by your average low-budget filmmaker: the independent festival movie and the B-movie exploitation film. Now, some people will claim these film genres are about as far apart as one can get, but I would propose the opposite. They are, in fact, the same.

Both usually explore areas that are somewhat taboo—say, alternative sex and violence. For example, an independent film might explore the relationship of two women in love and how they cope with the world around them. A B movie might deal with a female secret agent making love to her female counterpart in an effort to obtain the secret code that will avert a nuclear catastrophe. Now, I ask you, what's the difference?

Another similarity is cinematic technique. Both usually employ different cinematic techniques to convey their story. Perhaps the film will be shot in black-and-white or might utilize a handheld camera to give it a sense of urgency and the reality look that is so popular these days. These films will often emulate the style of the director's favorite film—most often, unsuccessfully.

Plot

Let's boil down your idea to its most basic element: the plot. The plot is your basic story line. Again, there are not a great deal of movies you can afford to make. I'm sure you have heard that old adage that there are only seven basic stories. Every story since the dawn of man has just been a variation on these seven basic stories. I'm not going to waste my time or yours arguing this point. There may be seven; then again, there might not be. But there is one thing that I can vouch for: There are only four basic stories that will make you money. And on top of that, there are five types of films that stand a good chance of getting into the majority of film festivals.

Take a look at a few basic story types and see if you have any of these elements in your idea.

The Bankable Four

1. The children's movie. No child can resist a cute, fluffy dog that befriends everybody and at the same time helps a dysfunctional family get back together while ridding the world of evil forces.

2. The gratuitous sex and bad comedy movie. This T&A movie can feature the young virgin on a quest to be laid or die trying. The lead character will face endless embarrassment, such as the hangover from hell when he discovers alcohol, or gratuitous beatings from the cool kids, all on the way to discovering his true identity.

3. The basic action movie. A down-on-his-luck guy with a bad reputation gets a phone call explaining that either his mother, father, spouse, or second cousin twice removed is in deep shit and only he can save the day. Our hero must fight against all the odds either to save the relative and get revenge on the bad guys, or to stop the hidden nuclear device from going off while promoting world peace and brotherly love.

4. The detective story. A gumshoe whose luck has run out gets an offer he cannot refuse for an easy job that turns impossibly complicated, and he subsequently becomes the target of a top-secret police investigation.

The Indie Five

1. Slackers talking in quick-witted Woody Allenesque dialogue updated for the twenty-first century.

2. The multiple-noun-titled movies. Examples include *Gas Food Lodging* and *Eat Drink Man Woman*. These movies often have nothing to do with their titles but for some reason they do have something to do with a couple of lost souls being visited by a stranger who shows them a whole new outlook on life.

3. The updated or blatantly ripped-off film from past film noir movie you rehash into something entirely new.

4. The gay indie film. It's like any other film, except a bunch of people are gay.

5. The "I shot this film on digital video and didn't use any lights or a tripod to keep it real" movie.

Now it's your turn to boil your story down into two or three sentences that will encapsulate your idea. This is your plot, and you should write it down because every scene you write and every word your characters breathe should in some way be connected to your plot. These three sentences are also very useful when somebody asks, "What is your film about?"

Plot Points

Once you have the spine of your story, you need a road map as to how the script will unfold. This road map is made up of plot points. A **plot point** is an action or event that spins your story off into a new direction. For example, say you pick basic story structure number two from the "Bankable Four" section. In this story, when the lead character jumps in his car and starts his three-thousand-mile drive to Mexico to get laid, that's a plot point. Say your lead character stops to buy gas in a small southern town. As he pumps his gas, he is accidentally mistaken for a mass murderer and thrown into the town lockup; that's another plot point. Here is the standard Hollywood formula: Your first plot point should occur around page 30, the second on page 90. That's it—two plot points per story. But in our screenplay, we are going to have a plot point every ten to fifteen pages (what we lack in money we will make up in plot points). Remember, more is better.

Characters

Now that you know your story, we need to talk about the characters. Your script is going to be character driven. No matter what type of film you choose to make, in one form or another, it will have the following cast of characters: the strong male or female lead, one sex interest, and three to five miscellaneous supporting characters. Hey, if you can make an interesting film with just one character, then go ahead. But you are going to have one hell of a time with the sex scenes and gunfights. Your characters must be instantly recognizable for what they are. The bad guys wear black. They have scarred faces and bad table manners. The good guys wear white and have perfect teeth, charming personalities, and the ability to break into song at any moment.

Here is a pool of stereotypical characters that should help you populate your script. Feel free to mix-and-match character traits to form a character that is pleasing to you.

Java. The down-on-his-luck cop given one last chance to redeem himself. Oftentimes, he is a trigger-happy alcoholic.

Scott. The slacker who has decided to try and find a job while not realizing that he is really in love with his best friend.

Angel. The hooker with a heart of gold, or the bad girl who wants to be good, or the good girl who want to be bad. Her only rule is that she never kisses anyone on the lips . . . unless she's in love.

Klondike. The sexy, yet sensitive, macho hero. Don't ask me to explain the contradiction; just remember, it's necessary.

Mr. Scaggs. The hit man who talks about the intricacies of fast food and all it has to offer society.

Moroflex. The scientist who can save the world and explain the more convoluted plot points in your script as elementary science to the viewing audience. This character is essential for revealing exposition that you cannot afford to shoot visually.

Franz. The nerdy, nervous guy who hangs out with the lead character to make the lead character look that much better. Franz usually has top-secret computer clearance.

Loopie. The crazy girl whom the hero lusts after because she is so full of life and vitality, but she is just a sham to teach our lead about the true meaning of love.

Charley. The strong female lead. She knows what she wants and usually gets it.

Thumper. The large, stupid man; sometimes he is mentally impaired, but he is always overweight. This character usually makes it to the end of the film, and then he is killed off at the last minute because the audience has grown sentimental toward this harmless, good-natured man. Use a name that is more befitting of a pet than a human. It's a nice touch.

Biff. The Izod-wearing, crew-cut jerk who assumes that date rape is a girl's idea of a good time. This character must always drive a convertible sports car. Also note that no high school or college movie can be made without this guy.

Mr. Smith. The bumbling authority figure, oftentimes supplying us with comic relief.

Russo. Our hero's sidekick. He has a tendency to talk in one-liners, providing the audience with comic relief. This funny guy will be tortured and then killed by the bad guys, giving our hero even more motivation to kick butt.

Remember that audiences like people they can recognize, and even the blind should be able to pick up on these oversimplified characters.

If you're feeling really adventurous, you can make up your own characters. Here is a quick-and-easy way to invent characters that may help you work out some of your pent-up hostilities at the same time. Invent characters based on *real* people. Say you need to invent a villain. First, make a list of all the jerks you know. Next, choose the jerk that has characteristics that match up to those you wish your villain to have. Now, think of an overexaggerated, grotesque caricature of this jerk. This is your character description, so write it down. Now, every time you have to write about this villain, just think about the person he is based on and what actions he would take under such circumstances. The best part comes when you have to kill him off. You should be able to save yourself thousands of dollars and years of psychological therapy with this writing technique. One important note: Remember not to use the person's actual name.

By the same token, you may be tempted to model somebody in your script after yourself—perhaps the hero who saves the world from certain destruction, or maybe the world's greatest lover. While this is certainly tempting, it can also be very dangerous. The first people who will view your film will be friends, family members, and significant others. Once they recognize which character is you, they might learn a little too much about the true you and begin to draw conclusions. If the character loves to needlepoint, don't be surprised if at Christmastime you receive a set of needles and miles of colored yarn. The other danger is you and your swelling head. Your ego could spin dangerously out of control. You might begin to believe that the superperfect person in the movie really is you. But what happens when you try to stop that jumbo jet with your pinky? OUCH! Reality will come crashing back in, albeit too late. And for that fleeting instant before you pass into the netherworld, you will realize that you had become an uncontrollable egomaniac.

First Scenes

The Action Movie

You have decided to make an exploitation B movie. Now, many people would turn up their noses and say you are wasting your time. I say bull. Movies are about escape, and nothing says escape better then a movie about a secret island inhabited by busty blondes and randy dinosaurs.

As far as I am concerned, there are only two possible scenes with which to start your movie. The first: a steamy-hot sex scene. You may want to consider lesbians for this one; they tend to grab the audience's attention very quickly. The second alternative: a murder. The more graphic and brutal, the better. And for those brave enough, how about a lesbian love scene that ends in murder (not recommended for the weakhearted).

The reason to start your movie this way is quite simple. You need something that is going to reach out to your audience, grab them by the neck, and yank them in. Nothing does it better then a set of 36 double Ds or a bullet through the head. There is no room here for the septuagenarian, rocking gingerly back and forth on his front porch, pining about his days as a shoe shiner to General MacArthur. People don't go to the movies to catch up on their sleep. People want stimulation, excitement, entertainment. Get it?

The Indie Film

The first scene in an indie sensation should also grab your audience. Even if you spend the next eighty minutes with your characters talking in a closet, you should at least try to suck the audience in with something interesting at the beginning. Remember that one of the primary outlets for the indie film is the myriad film festivals. When you submit your film to a festival, what is the first thing the screener sees? That's right, the first scene of your movie. The main thought here is getting into film festivals. Film festival committee members screen hundreds of films, and they quickly become jaded. Your job is to cut through the pile and rise to the top. The best way to do this is to make the first ten minutes as tight, clever, and compelling as possible.

Keep It Moving

Have you ever sat back in your movie seat and proceeded to count how many lightbulbs are in the ceiling? I can almost guarantee that this was not the reaction the filmmaker intended. No, these spot checks on light fixtures occur when the audience gets bored. This is most likely to happen somewhere between thirty to sixty minutes into your film. Don't make your audience crave content. Give it to them.

Your lead character is hot on the trail of the bad guys, but first he has to convey some crucial information to his partner—and to the viewing audience. Why? So we can marvel at the extreme cunning and superhuman powers of deduction your lead character possesses, he needs to discuss the facts with his partner/informer/friend who has top-secret computer clearance. To keep this very talky scene interesting, set it at a go-go bar. In fact, there is no better place for your characters to go than the local strip-o-rama. While your characters spew forth volumes of extraneous exposition, partially clad women can make love to fire poles. Just be careful to crosscut the images properly, or your audience won't pay attention and will complain later that they don't remember how the plot developed.

If you need an example of the importance of strip joints, rent *Beverly Hills Cop*, or *The Last Boy Scout*, or any other Tony Scott movie.

There are only three things that will keep your script moving: sex, murder, and action. Action is the most expensive of the three, so if your funds are limited, you might want to use this sparingly. Sex and murder are dirt cheap, and a liberal sprinkling of these throughout your film will go a long way toward ensuring its success. Let somebody else's film make the audience worry about the burned-out bulb all the way to the left, closest to the exit sign. Your audience won't be able to take their eyes off the screen.

Planting

Near the beginning of the script, your lead character is going to show the audience something. The secret is the way the character reveals this object. It has to be subtle enough that the audience doesn't think much of the item at the time, yet it must be obvious enough that the audience will remember it. This seemingly harmless object will come back later in your script to save the day. So, what is the object? It can be the gun left to him by his father, or the watch with the secret compartment containing a cyanide pill. The other importance of planting is that it lets your audience experience the "ah-ha" moment. This occurs when they figure out that the hero does indeed have a way out because he is armed with a Swiss Army watch. The most obvious form of planting can be found in any James Bond film. First Q introduces Bond and the audience to the new batch of toys he has whipped up in his secret workshop. Then, throughout the film, Bond will employ each of these props to get himself out of predicaments that would otherwise end in certain death. Thank goodness for the exploding dental floss!

 HINT: **This object is usually a weapon or tool of some sort.**

In revealing this object to our audience, be clever. It has to seem like an accident. It can fall out of our hero's mattress as he makes love to the blond bimbo. She will then find it and immediately question him about the object. It is then that our hero can explain the object has sentimental meaning: how his father gave it to him on his deathbed, or something similarly sappy.

 HINT: **If you attach some type of sentimental meaning to this object, it will be more powerful later when your hero uses it to dispatch the forces of evil.**

Have your hero tuck this tool safely away and continue on with your story like it has no meaning.

Later in the story when your hero is hanging by a thread, he will pull out this miracle weapon and save the day. By planting the object earlier in the script, you will avoid heckling comments from the viewing audience like "Where the hell did that come from?" or "How stupid!" or "Wasn't that convenient!"

Threes

That's right. Just like real life, in movies, things also must happen in threes. If you want your audience to remember anything, it has to happen at least three times.

That's right. Just like real life, in movies, things also must happen in threes. If you want your audience to remember anything, it has to happen at least three times.

That's right. Just like real life, in movies, things also must happen in threes. If you want your audience to remember anything, it has to happen at least three times.

Remember that America's scholastic skills are at an all-time low. If you expect your audience to have any retention, you will have to drive your point home with a sledgehammer. Never underestimate your audience's stupidity. Joe Schmo is not going to remember the significance of the solar flares unless you show him three times. Then he might understand that when the sun blows up everybody on the earth dies. Repetition is the key here.

Themes and Symbolism

Never worry about themes or symbolism. Just sit back and let them happen. Then smile when some pseudointellectual film buff compares your use of the candles in a dinner scene to the ape tossing the bone in *2001: A Space Odyssey*. These things are guaranteed to happen, so sit back and enjoy it.

Here are some other comments you might expect to hear: "The Christ imagery was ingenious" when you accidentally shot a cat's eye you made in camp in a bedroom scene; or "Your use of shadows has redefined film noir for the next millennium" when actually the truth is you could only afford two lights and one exploded as soon as you plugged it in. Or how about this one: "The handheld camera was true genius, no doubt ushering in a new age of cinema verité." The truth: You tried to save a few bucks on rentals that day and skipped on the tripod.

The Movie with a Message

Theme and message are different things. Every filmmaker has something to say. If you can integrate your message into your film without making it offensive or obvious, by all means do so. However, nobody likes a preachy lead character who, at any moment, is apt to lecture the audience on his views on the need to preserve the mating habits of the North American whooping crane. Nor do we want to hear that the world is an evil place and the only way out is to fight bad guys with really big machine guns while singing show tunes. Other overused messages include "Life is tough, so I'm gonna sit here on the couch with the TV remote." Or the all-too-popular "I am dying but it's OK because I have found inner peace." If you allow your message to bubble to the surface and become obvious to the audience, it will take away from both your film's entertainment value and perhaps your credibility as a filmmaker. So beware. Keep your urge to preach in check. You are a filmmaker, not a Scientologist–Moonie–Hare Krishna–Christian–Jewish–Jimmy Swaggart type.

Humor

This is the hardest aspect of writing the script. To be truly funny is rare. To be able to write comedy is even more difficult. People like to laugh, so if you can manage to integrate some humor into your script you will be that much better off. When your audience laughs, it is a sure sign that you as a filmmaker are connecting with them.

Now, don't have your characters tell Helen Keller jokes to each other; that's not comedy. In film, comedy can be either verbal—something the character says—or visual—something we see on screen—or a combination of both. Let's take any ZAZ (Zucker Abrahams Zucker) film—*Airplane*, for example. The jokes are piled high in this movie, but one device that is used repeatedly is the funny-weird-thing-in-the-background device. This comedic device works as follows. In the foreground, several characters will be discussing something, perhaps the end of the world or a similar topic. Meanwhile, the director will have a bit player or the comedic relief wrestling with a walking atomic bomb, oblivious to the fact that this evil device, which has now been given arms and a voice, could end the world at any moment. Any scene where Leslie Nielsen is in the background is probably an example of this comedic tool.

Other comedic events come from the unexpected. Think about *Raiders of the Lost Ark*. We all remember the scene in which Indy is confronted with the expert swordsman. We as an audience are prepared for a big fight, but no, Dr. Jones simply pulls out his gun and shoots the guy. That was unexpected, it was funny; and everybody remembers it.

Inside Humor

This is much easier. You should have at least one in-joke in your film. It can be either visual or verbal. An **in-joke** is something the cast and crew will recognize while screening the film. It is usually a reference to some event that happened during a late night of shooting when everybody was at their wit's end. This reference to the event will cause the cast and crew to laugh hysterically. Meanwhile, the rest of the people in the theater will not blink an eye but feel like they missed something. Oftentimes, they will laugh along. People are sheep.

The really great in-jokes just happen; you don't have to write them into your script. Remember that if you fail to get an in-joke you could always resort to the old standby—playing your outtakes during the title roll at the film's end.

One Location

One of the main considerations when writing the script is to make your movie economically feasible. Locations can greatly enhance the look and feel of your film. Windswept dunes or turquoise beaches or a fully operating space station will really add to the overall feel of your film. But this can get expensive; the fewer the locations, the cheaper the filming. Therefore, try to set the entire film around one locale. This is easier then you think. If the movie takes place in a house, you have a variety of rooms plus the grounds outside. Maybe there is a secret military installation in the basement—or, even better, there could be an underground bunker containing a Nazi U-boat.

Set Writing Goals

You should plan to write a minimum of five pages a day. As long as you keep moving forward, your script will be finished in twenty days. Just keep moving forward and don't worry if it makes sense. Just like the American automobile industry, we'll fix it later. Or even better, somebody will invent some type of aerosol spray called Script Doctor and sell it for just four easy payments of $9.99. And seeing as you probably watch a lot of late-night television, you might just pick it up.

By this time, you know your story, characters, and location. Now it's a simple matter of taking the information out of your mind and putting it down on paper. Your script will come in at exactly eighty-four pages. Do you find that constricting? Am I stifling your creative juices? Well, get used to it, because that's the way the world works. "But I heard that scripts for feature-length films are one hundred twenty pages." Stop whining; yes, they are. But you have neither the time nor the money nor, most important, the need for those extra forty pages (thirty-six for any mathematicians out there). In order for your film to be considered feature length, it must have a running time of eighty-four minutes. There is a standard formula (this is very complicated, so you might want to grab a calculator) to determine a film's length based on the screenplay.

One page of script = one minute of screen time

Now, here is a question for you: How many minutes will an eighty-four-page script run?

Right! Eighty-four minutes.

Using this formula, it becomes quite clear why our script will be the specified length. Don't worry if it comes in a little short. A slow-crawling title roll can add minutes to your film.

Index Cards

A good way to plan your movie is to write down ideas for scenes on index cards. One scene per card. When you get about thirty cards, you should have enough scenes to fill out a feature-length screenplay. Now, before you get too excited about stringing together thirty random scenes, we need to discuss structure.

How many times have you walked out of a theater ready to slit your wrists while uttering the words "That made no sense!" This is a reaction that you as a filmmaker do not want from your audience. You want your audience to exclaim "That was so clever," or "That's the best film I've ever seen, and I see a lot of films." These comments are uttered for films that have a logical structure. The structure of your film should go something like this: One scene flows into the next, helping to build and explain the story until its conclusion.

Right now, go to the local office superstore for a fresh pack of index cards. If you want to get really nifty, you might buy a pack of rainbow-colored ones. Then you can use a separate color for each type of scene. No side trips on the way home; we've got a movie to build here. I'll wait here, but hurry because they're going to close soon.

Great, you're back. On the first card, write your first scene—this is where your story will begin. On the next card, jot down the last scene—yup, this is the ending. Now spread these two cards about seven feet apart. At one-foot intervals, we are going to insert five more cards; these are going to contain the plot points that we discussed above. The last step is to fill in the empty space between these cards with scenes that allow the characters to get from one plot point to the next.

Writing out scenes on individual cards gives you the flexibility to move scenes around and see how they work in different contexts. You can rearrange them until you find the right order. Spread the cards out on your living room floor and find the order that works best for your story. You might need to add in a new card to make your story flow better, or you might find a card out of place. Either way, it's OK to add and subtract cards.

Once you settle on a sensible order, keep the cats or small children away and carefully stack the cards, first scene on top and last scene on the bottom. Good job. Now tap your index finger three times on the top cards while uttering the words *first draft*. Look back at your little pile and tell me what you see. If you still see a little pile of cards, get yourself over to the computer and fire that sucker up. If you see anything that resembles a dragon or a snake, try and get some sleep (you might also want to think about a detox program). If you have actually conjured a dragon, then write a film about your magic powers and become a gazillionaire.

Begin typing. Your hands should be running over the keyboard at an astronomical rate. Just think, each word you type brings you that much closer to your completed script. Try to expand each card into a complete scene that runs two to three pages. Grab the next card and keep writing. Before you know it, you will have a feature-length screenplay.

Hold on a second. I got a little ahead of myself. Take a moment to think about the people who will inhabit your screenplay. As you craft your scene, you also need to craft the personalities and traits of these people. You would be surprised how much a little character flaw can tell your audience about a character. Flaws are also good because the audience can sympathize with flawed characters; after all, the audience is human, and all humans have flaws, don't they?

Writer's Block

OK, you're cruising along. You've got about forty pages down and—bang!—you run into a brick wall. Your mind has gone blank. You feel like you have been **degaussed,** a film term for erasing videotape. Hey, don't worry about it. Now is the perfect time for your character to pull out a gun. And since it's out, why not have him kill somebody? This should spin your story off into a new direction, and the ideas should come flowing back.

For example, you can now introduce the wife of the dead man. Have your lead character take her to bed. Oh, but her jealous sister enters the room while they are in the act. *Is this easy or what?* Reluctantly, she joins them (potential lesbian scene). They decide to work together, but the sister is really working for the bad guys.

The possibilities are endless. Just don't be afraid to involve your characters in murder or unsafe sex, and your movie will be a winner.

Your Audience

It is very important that you understand movie audiences. They come in several very distinct categories.

The quiet people. This is your invisible audience; because they are unobtrusive, they are often not counted.

The slaphappys. These people will clap wildly when something pleases them. You don't want to sit next to them because their wildly flaying hands might smack you.

The talkers. These people actually talk to the screen. They believe that by pointing out to the hero that a bad guy is hiding in the bushes with a gun, he will then be able to take the appropriate action. They think they are the only members of the viewing audience who can see the twenty-foot gun barrel on the movie screen. Without them, the moment would undoubtedly pass by the rest of the audience.

The laughers. These people want to laugh, and they won't let even the stupidest movie jokes stand in their way.

The know-it-all film students. These guys are looking at what's out there, what's new, what's happening. Like it or not, they are grading your film and deciding mentally whether they could do it better.

The lawyer and his wife, the fashion designer. She doesn't really make a living at her job and he is going to charge you a hundred fifty bucks just to pick up the phone and talk to you, so who cares what they think about your film. Just make sure you make them your friends, so he will charge you only for the actual time he is working on your behalf and not for the time he is on the golf course.

Pickups and shotguns. These action-oriented, shit-kicking, ditch-digging, beer-swilling, 4 × 4–driving filmophiles will make up the bulk of your film's audience. And believe me, they know a good piece of bad film when they see it. Campy is OK; but beware, if your film takes its ridiculous plot too seriously, your audience will sense it and might become vicious, like rabid dogs. They will pick your story apart. So keep your sense of humor.

Film festival groupies. These sushi-loving, film-digesting bohemians want to see movies. Sure, they have been dele-

gated to the little art house across town with the crappy projector, ripped seats, and an espresso machine in the concession stand instead of the artificial popcorn butter-dispensing
pump. But all this has simply hardened their resolve. Once
they have entered the theater, they will give you the benefit
of the doubt. If you confuse them, they will give you even
more time.

A Few Movies to Rent to Get You into the Mood

The idea here is to go down to the video store and pick out titles
that will make you feel good. Films that your dog and his cat
friends could make better. Skip the A titles and the new releases.
That's right, keep moving back, past the drama section, past the
foreign section, keep on going. If you pass through those black
curtains you have gone too far, but you are probably in the right
neighborhood. Ah, there it is, cult and schlock B titles. What we're
looking for is box covers with catchphrases such as "Straight Outta
Hell" or "Dripping Blood." Longer campy titles are also good. Rent
a few of these movies, get some nuclear popcorn, and sit down and
enjoy yourself. You will be amazed at the garbage that gets distributed these days. And you will find yourself saying, "I can do
that." Don't forget to rewind the tapes.

 HINT: **Now that you are a filmmaker, you may be able to
claim video rentals as a tax deduction.**

Endings

The Last Scene of a B Movie

You have the opening of your movie. Now you need to know the ending. What happens at the climax of your film? Again, there are very few options open to you. First off, somebody has to win. Americans love a winner. A film that does not have a clear-cut winner will force its audience to actually think, and that's the last thing they want to do. Many foreign films go the ambiguous-ending route. Believe me, you don't want to go that way. So remember, either the good guy or the bad guy wins.

In your movie, you must have good guys and bad guys. You have neither the time nor the money to examine the frailties of a character who is caught in the middle and cannot make the proper choice between good and bad, light and dark, Coke and Pepsi. In short, no "OK guys" will populate your screenplay. If one tries to slip in, just kill him off. Save yourself a headache and give the audience a cheap thrill at the same time.

The second thing that you have to decide is who gets the girl.

HINT: **The person who wins can usually lay claim to the buxom blonde; for example, slay the dragon, then lay the bimbo.**

Now, some of you female readers might take offense at that hint. But it serves a double purpose. You see, by offending you, I might get some free publicity for this book. When you arrive at your local bookstore draped in sandwich boards plastered with clever rhyming slogans, people are going to want to know what the stink is about. They will buy this book to find out. So relax; in your screenplay, the strong-willed female can destroy the forces of evil and lay claim to the surfer dude with the incredible mane of blond hair, the great pecs, and the inability to understand even the simplest fast-food restaurant menus.

Finally, what does your character achieve on a global scale? You have to make your movie important to the average man. That means your plot must have global implications; an outcome that quite possibly could affect Joe Moviegoer and his miserable life working as a bathroom attendant at an all-you-can-eat Mexican restaurant. He will become more involved in your story if, in the back of his mind, he makes the connection that if the bad guys blow up the nuclear reactor he will no longer be able to heat up his frozen burrito at the local quickie mart.

So what will it be? Save the world from the poisonous nerve gas, stop the bad guys from raiding the World Bank, or save the world from the Mutant Broccoli People? The possibilities are endless. The key word here is *world*. As long as you include this word in your description, everything will be fine. As an exercise, fill in this blank:

Your hero saves the *world* from _____.

The Indie Film Ending Scene

The end of an indie film can take many forms. Sometimes it can be the anti-ending that flies in the face of convention. Sometimes it can be the beginning of the film, but shown at the end. In the indie film genre, the audience expects something other than the traditional ending. Don't upset them with the long-kiss-on-the-beach-as-the-sun-sets-behind-them ending.

False Endings

You're sitting in the theater, the film ends, you grab your coat and begin to walk out to beat the rush, but then you realize the film isn't actually over. What just happened? The dreaded false ending. You were sure that when the hero dispatched the villain and rode off into the sunset, the film was over. But no, it keeps on going. The hero returns home, cooks a meal, checks his e-mail, and so on. Why? Who knows. All I know is, the audience wanted to leave and most of them probably already have when the film comes to a logical ending. The false ending should be avoided.

Even worse is the double false ending. The only exception to this rule is if you are making a horror movie. In this genre, audiences expect—no, *demand*—the false ending, because they know that you have one final scream to eke out of them before they leave the theater to experience the horror of trying to remember where they parked their cars.

The Big Ending

Any film can have the so-called big ending and your audience will appreciate it, that's for sure. Since the dawn of cinema, movies have ended with a bang. From Fred Ott's *Sneeze* to the exploding death star, movies have always ended in a bang. Make sure you include one at the end of your film. It can be a car chase, a shoot out, a nuclear explosion, or the orgasm to end all orgasms coinciding with the apocalyptic end of the world. Without the big ending, you are cheating your audience. Audiences always remember filmmakers who don't deliver the goods. So make sure you have included the big finish in your script.

There, you have everything you need to get your script ready. Happy writing. See you at page 84.

chapter 3

What does it take to make a feature film?

C ome on, you know the answer to this one. That's right, money. To get money so you can make your film you are going to need to hit the street running. You are going to live, eat, and sweat film. Every time you get the desire to plop down on the couch and watch a little television, *Don't.*

Be warned: There is perhaps nothing more relaxing or soothing than watching Bob Ross posthumously paint with his selection of knives uttering, "This happy little tree is going to live here" and "It's your world, do what you want." Net result? A day lost. Even worse, if you munch down a bag of potato chips before nodding off, you might just be out of commission for the next day, too. So let's make an agreement. Grasp this book in your right hand and hold up your left hand. Now repeat after me: "I am going to be ruthless in my search for the financial means to make my feature film a reality. Furthermore, I promise not to watch any painting shows on PBS, especially the white guy with the big afro who paints with knives. So help me D. W. Griffith." Good. Now, let's go find some cash.

Financing

How much is this movie going to cost? Should I wait until I have the full amount of money to begin shooting my film? How come all these sections start with questions? Just read the book, would you, and save the petty criticisms for the critics.

At this level of filmmaking, the most crucial financial question is: Will I be shooting my feature film on motion-picture film or on videotape? This chapter assumes you have chosen film. Chapter 8, "Digital Video," covers the other side of the question. Either way, read on, because no matter what format you are shooting on, some costs just cannot be avoided.

Let's make a budget to get an idea of how much filmmaking is going to cost financially. As far as the deep emotional costs incurred by this experience, I'm afraid that is up to you and your psychiatrist. When making a low-budget feature film, your biggest expense is film stock. Assume that you shoot at a ratio of 3:1, meaning that for every minute of actual screen time in your finished film you will shoot three minutes of film on location. What happens to the other two-thirds of the film that gets shot? Well, some will be used up by blown takes when the actors flub a line or miss a mark. The bulk will go toward additional coverage so that you have editing choices for when you cut the film together. A small amount will be the waste at the head and tail of each reel of film.

Film Stock

Time for more math. Don't worry, there won't be a test. A 400-foot can of 16-mm film runs for 11 minutes. Your film is 84 minutes long, so you will need 8 cans of film to make your feature film. But remember you are shooting at a 3:1 ratio, so multiply the 8 by 3 and now you have 24. That is the actual number of film cans (with film inside of them) that you will need to purchase in order to make your feature film. If you can manage to pick up these cans at $75 a pop, it will cost you $1,800 to buy the proper amount of film stock.

Next you need to develop the film and either transfer it to videotape or make a film daily. Either way it will cost about the same. If you shop around, you should be able to get the film developed and transferred to video for approximately $2,700. I am giving you $1,200 for developing and $1,500 for your video dailies.

Food

You are going to be shooting for ten days, so let's assume you will need to spend $70 per day on food and drink. That makes for a food budget of $700. Using some coupons and shoving some items inside other items to try to fool the cashier could save $200. Grand total for food: $500. Let me be clear. I am not advocating stealing. I'm advocating cutting costs.

Equipment

Film equipment includes the camera, the lights, and either a digital audiotape (DAT) or a Nagra sound recorder. When it comes to procuring film equipment, there are a couple of ways you can go. First there are rental houses; unfortunately for you, they are in business to make money. That means that for each piece of equipment you want to rent they are going to charge you a fee. Also working against your budget is the fact that they will require you to purchase insurance in case you drop their camera off a cliff. On top of all that, they will charge you tax. Now, if you rent a camera for a couple of hundred dollars a day and a few lights at twenty a pop and then a DAT recorder and slate for a hundred or so bucks a week, you will pretty quickly run up a bill for thousands of dollars. Luckily for you, there are other ways to lay your hands on the necessary equipment, and most of them do not involve running at high speed with uniformed men in pursuit.

Another and probably better (for the purposes of this example *better* means *cheaper*) option is to hire a director of photography and a soundman who own their equipment. The advantages to this approach are many. First, if you can find an eager, up-and-coming director of photography who is frothing at the mouth for the opportunity to light and shoot his first feature film, he might just do it for nothing. Then again, he might charge you for the use of his camera equipment. Keep in mind, the more eager he is, the cheaper you should be able to negotiate the rental price on his equipment. Ask about the package price. Work out one flat fee for the camera rental and include the option for a day or two of pickup shots or reshoots as part of the fee. Another advantage to this approach is that it will save the cost of getting equipment insured. Also, if you end up paying your cameraman in cash—and believe me, camera people love cash—you will save sales tax on the rental and contribute nothing to Uncle Sam and our dwindling economy. If you rent your equipment from a rental house or if you have a crew member bring it along, limit yourself to no more than $1,200.

Expendables

Your characters are going to need clothing and props, so budget $200 for this. You are also going to need something called expendables. **Expendables** are anything you use and then throw out, such as gaffer's tape or lighting gels. Gaffer's tape you must buy. Gels, on the other hand, can be accumulated in a variety of ways. The number one method is going through the garbage of a bigger budget shoot. For this shoot, limit your expendables to $100.

Editing

The next major expense is going to be editing. This involves two things: the editor and the editing equipment. If you already own a computer, you can borrow some software and set up your own editing system quite inexpensively. If you don't, find somebody who owns the equipment and will either edit it for free or let you use the equipment. Either way, budget $2,000 for editing.

Sound

Finally, the cost of your sound mix and Automatic Dialogue Replacement (ADR) is going to run $1,000.

Miscellaneous

Keep in mind that this budget doesn't include all the little tidbits that always cost an extra buck. You might need a prop here, or a small rodent for atmosphere there. So let's add another $424.99 under Miscellaneous.

Here is your film's budget. As this book's title promises, it is under $10,000.

Film stock	$1875.00
Food	500.00
Equipment	1,200.00
Props and wardrobe	200.00
Expendables	100.00
Developing	1,200.00
Video transfer	1,500.00
Edit	2,000.00
Sound and Mix	1,000.00
Miscellaneous	424.99
TOTAL	**$9,999.99**

You might have noticed there is no money in the budget for paying crew and talent. This is a rule you are going to have to stick to. Nothing can decimate funds faster than actually paying people. Besides, if you are working for free, why shouldn't everybody else?

This budget is going to allow you to shoot a film, edit it, and have a high-quality video copy available for screening.

Already, we are up to $10,000 and we haven't even included sales tax. Now trick yourself into believing that you really can make a feature film for under $10,000. Then, once you've spent the first $10,000, you will be in too deep to stop. This is how the major studios operate, so don't feel bad when you have to come up with additional funds.

A film is much like an illegitimate child. It will take lots of money—*your* money. A lot of other people will spend time with it as well. But on weekends and at night, you may be able to spend some time with it. You will spend endless hours working menial jobs to support it. In the end, you will know that you were responsible for it, and you have to accept it for what it is. Unlike a child, once you finish a film, you can stick it in a closet and not worry about going to jail.

Ten People

Remember all those friends you made in college? Well, right now they are employed; some might be investment bankers, others doctors and lawyers. That's right, they have respectable jobs and are making a contribution to society. Think about the possibilities here. If you can get ten people together and squeeze them for $1,000 each, well, guess what? You just got your budget! The standard formula for raising money by selling off shares goes like this: Split the film in half. Fifty percent will be sold to investors to raise the capital needed to produce your film. The second 50 percent you keep as your share. From this share you might have to give away **points**, or a percentage, to certain key crew members and actors to secure their involvement. Don't be afraid to sell off shares of your film to get much needed capital. Better yet, get individuals who are not only interested in investing, but also in helping out with the shoot. With their own money on the line, they will work doubly hard.

Don't Expect One Cent from Any Living Relative

While everybody in your immediate family will marvel how exciting it must be to make a movie, they will also be calling their accountants to make sure no unauthorized transfers of funds take place. When push comes to shove, don't expect any money from the living. The dead, however, are entirely different. Now, I'm not saying don't try to tap the family tree. Try to chop it down if you want. Just be prepared for the worst. But before you run out to shake the family tree, let's draw the line in the sand. Nobody should force anybody in their family to take a mortgage out on their house in order to finance a film. Films are highly speculative, and you're going to feel really bad when Granny winds up living in a remodeled refrigerator box in Central Park because she graciously decided to take a mortgage out on her condo to finance your dreams.

Credit Cards

We have all heard the stories about people financing their feature films with credit cards. But will it really work? Sure it will, but you will create a mountain of debt. Also, finanacing with credit cards is a publicity trick that has already been done, so try and think up your own absurd way of paying for your movie. I would only use credit cards as a last resort. Remember, if worse comes to worst, you can say, "I'll use the card." How about using somebody else's charge card? Did you know that today a myriad of film products can be ordered over the phone and shipped to your door? Do your parents look through their credit card bills? Would they notice a $2,000 charge from Eastman Kodak? Can't you throw the bill away before they get it? Do you have a criminal record? These are questions you need to ask yourself. However, you should know that in the age of prison overcrowding, the court system treats first-time offenders very leniently. Picking up litter next to the interstate is not a big price to pay for a freezer full of film stock.

Las Vegas

Rooms are cheaper at midweek. Bet the *don't pass line* at the craps table. Start your bets off at $25 a round and work your way up to $100. If you have a good night, you could leave with your film's budget. If you lose . . . well, you had a good time and everyone around will think you're a big shot. Either way, you've won. Here is the craps table layout and proper bet placement.

Craps Table
Place your bets on the Don't Pass line.

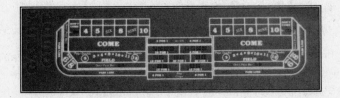

That's it.

One more thing: avoid the Native American–run casinos. Usually the odds of winning are less at these establishments. I once lost about three film budgets at one of them.

Garage Sale

How important is this film to you? Well, if it's very important, you might want to consider having a yard sale. That's right. Get rid of all those distracting worldly possessions. Lead a simple life. You can easily generate enough money to shoot a film by selling off all those capitalist luxuries you have worked so hard to accumulate over the years. Remember, save the coffeemaker. You will need this on the set.

Marry Rich

It may be time to find that wealthy girl or guy and get married. Then you can slowly kill her or him with rat poison or apple seeds. You come out of this deal with the money *and* the story for your feature film. Not bad. But seriously, in order to marry a rich girl, you need to meet a rich girl and have her fall in love with you. Not as easy as it sounds. I've been to so many debutante balls, I have a Lester Lanin tattoo.

Selling Credits

Here's an idea that will bring out the businessperson inside of you. You can make a list of film credits such as grip, gaffer, associate producer, and so on. Next to each credit put a price. Of course, the better the credit, the more it costs. You could sell the associate producer credit for $250, which would be the high end, a production assistant credit could go for as little as twenty bucks. There is no reason every crew member couldn't sell at least five of these credits. At the very least, your older sisters and brothers will buy a credit.

> *USELESS FILM FACT:* **Most filmmakers were born the youngest child.**

Get creative. For $25, how about letting people make up their own credits? While you won't get your entire budget this way, you might come up with some much-needed petty cash.

Things are going pretty well at this point. You should have a little cash in your pocket. You've finished your script and are going over it, adding just the right touches. Now, let me introduce you to the cast of real-life characters whom you will have to share a condo with in Park City if your film is fortunate enough to get accepted in a festival there.

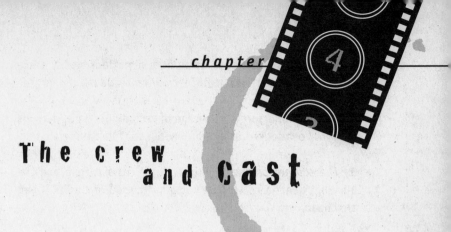

The crew and cast

ou should be able to make your film with a crew of six or seven fully functional human beings with IQs in the eighty-plus range. These nameless people are going to have specific jobs and responsibilities.

Your crew will consist of the following:

1. _The director_ (no explanation needed).

2. _The producer_ supplies the money for the shoot, deals with contracts, and handles all the other logistical aspects of the film. Oftentimes on a lower-budget film, the producer and the director are the same person. There is a very easy test to find out if you are both the producer and the director. Look at your bank account. Have you spent money on photocopying scripts or renting casting space? If the answer is yes, you are the producer.

3. _The director of photography_ **(DP)** is the person in charge of lighting the set, operating the camera, and helping the director transfer his or her vision onto film. He is also the person who holds the light meter—more on this later.

4. *The soundperson* is in charge of recording sound, perhaps the most overlooked aspect of low-budget filmmaking.

5. *The camera assistant* is in charge of the camera and the film that goes in it. This may also be the job of the DP if you are cheap.

6. *The swing guy* is in charge of everything nobody else wants to be in charge of. Despite the title, the swing guy rarely agrees to cross-dress at parties or makes passes at you. Rarely.

7. *The production assistant* (**PA**) is in charge of the film's petty cash. This person will often need to buy beer and cheap furniture from IKEA to furnish the set. Additionally, the PA can be a film's greatest asset. A couple of motivated guys can really help out when you need something in a hurry.

The first four people are crucial. If you can, get all seven.

The key to managing your crew is this: Give everybody in your crew very specific responsibilities so that when somebody screws up you will know who to blame. Then realize it doesn't matter who you blame because, ultimately, you as the director are going to rise or fall on this piece of work, not the guy who was supposed to buy an indigo throw pillow but instead came back with a teal babushka.

Director

The director will be running the set. He is in charge of working with the actors and getting their performances right. The director will also set up the shot; hopefully, with the help of the DP. The director has the final say on everything that happens on set and on any other creative decisions.

Here are a few questions you can expect to hear and must be able to answer if you are going to be a successful director.

Do you like this shade of teal or would the sea foam be better?

I don't understand why I say this line. Could we take a moment to read through the scene together?

We ran out of money for dinner. Should we serve yesterday's leftover pasta mixed with the extra lunchmeat from today's lunch, or should we charge something to your credit card?

This film would look great if we shot the whole thing at sunset. That gives us about an hour of shooting time per day. What do you think?

Why should I take my clothes off for you?

When somebody asks you, the director, a question, you had better have an answer. The two best responses are "yes" and "no." "Maybe" or "I don't know" suck. They make you seem wishy-washy. You are the leader of this motley bunch, so take charge. It's either a yes or a no. But be nice, because when you're not paying anybody, it makes it real easy for them to walk away. And the last thing you want is to become a one-man film crew.

Producer

You, as the producer, will need to find the money to produce the film. It can be yours, or it can come from a drug lord; but one way or another, you have to have the cash. Now, we all know that the person with the cash also pays for the bill at the restaurant. This is another task for the producer. You must wine and dine those you deem necessary for the successful completion of your film. I would put the emphasis on wine, and if you buy it by the box, you might be able to get people in the right frame of mind to participate in your feature-film venture. Just remember: Don't take Tylenol for your hangover, and be sure to drink plenty of water before you go out for the night.

Director of Photography

This position must be filled by someone who is competent and has some visual sense. Vito from the local garage will not do. The director of photography will be in charge of lighting each scene. He will also operate the camera, so he must have some concept of framing. The director of photography is also in charge of the technical crew, which is composed of the assistant cameraman, the gaffer, and the electricians, as well as the grips. (I know that I didn't mention a gaffer or electricians before. But much like the process of filmmaking itself, I continually change the playing field. By the time you finish your film, you will have a crew of hundreds.)

Finding a Director of Photography

The best way to audition a DP is to first take a look at something called a **reel**, a compilation tape that every DP puts together to demonstrate his or her work. Keep in mind that your candidates are only showing their best work, so a reel should look good. The other aspect of screening a reel is to find a DP who has a style that you like. It would also be a good idea to let any potential candidate know what type of look you are going for on your film. You can find many DPs advertising in the classified sections of any of the independent filmmaking magazines. Also, there are people known as **DP reps** whose sole purpose in life is to match you, the up-and-coming filmmaker, with their clients, the up-and-coming DPs. These reps might try to hit you in the pocketbook, but if you cannot afford their clients, at the very least you will be able to screen several reels and get a feeling for who and what is out there.

Once you have decided on a couple of potential DP candidates, set up meetings. Go to your local java joint and sit with them for a while; it is here that you will test your ability to live with them for the next month.

Remember when you went off to summer camp with your best friend from third grade? Well, after four weeks of pink bellies, wedgies, wiener roasts, and finally the color war, you hated his guts, didn't you? Filmmaking is a lot like sleepaway camp—and yes, you will get an opportunity to raid the girls' bunk. Just don't get caught.

DP Framing Test

Here is a DP IQ test. Have any potential directors of photography choose the pictures they believe are framed properly.

The Framing Test

SCORING THE TEST

6 correct = Qualified to operate the camera on your film.

5 correct = If the candidate is recovering from a late night out, you might overlook this one mistake.

3–4 correct = Close, but keep looking.

1–2 correct = Legally blind and shouldn't be operating anything, much less a camera.

0 correct = Avant-garde filmmaker; immediately ship off to France.

Sound Guy

You would think that anybody who can work a VCR should be able to record sound on a set. Do you know how hard it is to get the clock to stop blinking twelve o'clock? Well, sound work is just as maddening. The sound guy's job is to record the dialogue at the highest possible level without overmodulating while simultaneously minimizing background noise. Make sure your sound guy is good, or your film might not be.

Camera Assistant

This is also a crucial position. This person will be in charge of the camera. That means loading the film magazines, cleaning those big hairs out of the gate, keeping track of film stock, pulling focus, and all the other chores associated with the ·camera. Anal-retentive people make very good camera assistants, so think about those extratidy, uptight people you know. It's as good a place to start as any.

Swing Guy

This crew member will take care of all the odd jobs that crop up. He may be pushing the dolly on one shot or panning a light on another. It is always preferable to have an extra set of hands available. This position is the most thankless of all seven, so be as nice as possible when you ask him to drive two thousand miles back to your apartment to pick up the battery belt.

Production Assistant

This is not your coffee boy. A good production assistant can do everything from breaking into cars to scheduling shoot days to conning a storeowner into letting you shoot in his or her store for free. The thing to remember is that every production assistant is an aspiring director, so in addition to helping you with your film, the PA is also plotting and planning how to make his or her own. Some crew members might even go beyond the talking stage.

The Crew You May or May Not Have

Gaffer

Let's start with the **gaffer**. He is the head electrician and works directly under the DP. When the DP devises a lighting scheme for a set, he will pull the gaffer aside and tell him what kind of lights he wants and where they should go. The gaffer then breaks up the task and distributes it to individual electricians, telling them where to run cables and place the lighting units. If the film has a small crew, it will usually be up to the DP and the gaffer to get the lights where they need to go.

Key Grip

The **key grip** is the counterpart to the gaffer. He is the leader of the grip team. Grips are in charge of rigging things. They place flags, build other rigs to block out light, and are often very handy with rope and tools. If you need something fixed at your house, invite a grip over. Basically, the gaffer and the electrician are responsible for making light, and the grips are responsible for taking light away or channeling it.

More Crew

We have all seen the **assistant director (AD)** credit scroll past during a film's closing credits. What do you suppose this person is responsible for? The AD is responsible for the day-to-day operations of the set. This means that he tells everybody else on the set where to go and when to go there; this includes bringing the right actors to the set at the right time.

The **production designer** is responsible for the look of the film; on a no- or low-budget film, the production designer will also be responsible for props. Props are important, so make sure you have somebody in charge of gathering them up before you shoot.

As you know, some films have an endless crew list with jobs that oftentimes defy understanding. Rest assured that you can do any of these jobs yourself if it is absolutely necessary, but ideally you would like to concentrate on directing your film. Try to delegate as much as possible.

Right-Hand Man

You now have to assemble your crew. Start by getting just one other person to work with you: a right-hand man. You will be amazed at how much easier everything will become if you have another carbon-based biped to bounce your ideas off. So go visit your best pal, or the guy you go to drive-in movies with, or that friend who is always adjusting the color on your TV. Tell him what you plan to do. Then ask him for his help, and don't take no for an answer. Yes, you might need to bribe him, but that's OK. What else are friends for?

Wow! Things are really moving now. You have just doubled the size of your production company. With your trusty companion, it's time to take your script and try to find the real-life bodies that will occupy the characters that you have so carefully constructed.

Let's Get This Party Started

The script is done. Or at least you think it is. In fact, it will never be done. Even after you shoot your film. So don't worry if your script is not perfect; it's a working blueprint. You need actors, a crew, locations, and equipment, not to mention wardrobe, props, film stock, and all the other items associated with filmmaking that usually take a crew a hundred weeks to assemble at an astronomical cost. You are now going to take on this huge logistical task, which people have compared to a military operation, and you are going to do it for almost no money and no access to stealth technology.

Casting

The first thing you are going to do is get the word out. So get in your car and head to town. You can read the rest of this chapter when you get stuck in traffic. Remember, it's OK to read in traffic, but just don't pull out the cell phone to make a call or you might get a ticket.

Your first stop is going to be the local paper. If you live in New York City, you are in the subway heading toward 42nd Street to place an ad in *Backstage*. If you are in Los Angeles, you have an excuse not to get into your car. You can phone your add into *Drama-Logue* or one of the other local casting newspapers. If you're anywhere in between these two cities, you are on your way to the local paper.

Place an ad announcing that you are casting a motion picture. In the ad, give a brief description of the plot, the characters, and what you are offering in return to any potential actor. I would offer meals, transportation, and a copy of the movie. Also, provide an address where prospective actors and actresses (I believe as of this writing that both male and female actors are known as actors, actually) can mail their headshots and résumés. If you live in a very small town, it might be advisable to hit more than one paper. Also, spin by any local theater groups and drop off a slip of paper with the same info. This way a local thespian or two may come your way.

The Most Popular Guy on the Block

You know your casting ads have hit the papers because your mailman seems to be leaning sharply to the left. This is because of the extra fifty pounds of headshots he is carrying in his bag, thanks to you. If your ad was a great success, or if you offered money, you should expect a three- to four-foot pile of nine-by-twelve manila envelopes. This applies to New York and Los Angeles only. If you live in the outskirts, be happy with a one-foot pile. If you get too much mail, your mailman might bring it to you in a mailbag, just like the way Santa gets his mail—except, instead of "Ho ho ho," you'll hear a whole bunch of expletives.

 HINT: **One foot of headshots equals one hundred submissions.**

Wait a few days until the mail peters down to a trickle, then get ready to swing into action. First, gather your dirty laundry together and place it near the door. Second, call your associate over and start ripping the envelopes open. Sort the headshots into piles. One pile will be for the potential candidates for each part. You will also build two other piles. The first will be for those who don't have a chance for anything, the second, for those who you will never use but you will keep around because they are hilarious. As you sort through the submissions, you will find a sprinkling of cards and letters from people offering other services to you, such as composers who would like to do the music for your film, film labs, equipment rental houses, and editors. Keep these; they may come in handy later. When you are finished, take the pile marked "Not a Chance for Anything," bundle it up, and stick it next to the fireplace as kindling. Next, take the funny ones and put them in a safe place.

You should have an individual pile for each part you need to cast. By carefully scrutinizing each headshot and the attached résumé, cut each pile down to no more than twenty possible candidates. Those are the people you will be calling in to meet personally.

> *HINT:* **Don't throw away the headshots and résumés from the other potential candidates for each role; you might not be happy with the first twenty candidates.**

Bundle up all your potential candidates and place them next to your dirty laundry.

Casting Call

Now drive to your parents' house, and don't forget to bring your laundry and the headshots. While your clothes are in their washing machine, you are going to use your parents' phone to call up all those people—or, I should say, call their phone answering services. That's right. You're not going to get a home answering machine, you're going to get something called an answering service, which will forward your message to the actor you have called. Seems like actors are one of the last groups of people on the planet to embrace the answering machine. Sure they have one, but they would rather you call some kind of phone answering service instead. Why? Because actors are quirky people.

Once you get a person or answering service or machine or whatever on the other end of the phone line, leave the following information. First, remind the candidate about your film project. Then leave information about the time and date that you would like to meet with that person. After about twenty calls, throw your wash into the dryer. As you leave, swipe a handful of those clothespins your mother uses to hang the laundry out to dry. Make sure they are the spring-clip type.

No sooner have you made your first round of calls than your

prospective actors will begin ringing your phone. The first ones to call are usually actors who can't make the time and date you have set up for their casting call. You can try to accommodate their requests by changing times, but I would not change days for anyone.

The Talent

Everybody wants to be in a movie. You will meet two types of people as you continue along on your quest to cast your feature: those who immediately assume you are making a porno film, and know that they should have a part (even though they are short, bald, and probably can't get it up); and those who truly know what it means to be an actor. Those who know usually come with some type of reading material under their arm.

Novices really don't know how long it takes to make a film. Therefore, if you cast them, beware. Tell them they must prepare themselves for long days, sleepless nights, and bad food. If they seem unfazed, then they might be usable. If they waver, cut them loose and save yourself the aggravation. You cannot afford to lose an actor halfway through the shoot. That would require rewriting the script.

Attitude is almost as important as acting ability. Sure it would be nice if actors could cry on cue, but that's nothing a little saline solution can't fix. But try dealing with a prima donna who demands special fruit cups and organic plates that carbon-date back to Neanderthal man. These people are truly a pain in the ass—and they shoot your food budget through the roof. So pick people you can get along with, and make sure they can get along with you.

Auditions

Don't be afraid to have the actors come to your home to read the lines. Sure, some may be overzealous, but the odds are pretty good that they won't kidnap the dog to get the part. When they arrive, have a small waiting area set up that is devoid of all valuables and breakables—that means your mother's prized collection of *Beauty and the Beast* commemorative plates need to be hidden. Have separate piles with pages for each part laid out so the actors can pick up a copy of their respective lines. You might want to type out a little bio on each character to further assist them. In the industry, these are known as **sides** and **character breakdowns**. Some actors might ask you if sides will be available. They are not asking about mashed potatoes and coleslaw from the local KFC.

Bring the actors in one at a time and talk to them about the movie. Tell them when you will be shooting. Get a feel for what type of people they are. Also be aware that they are trying to be extremely friendly toward you. After all, they want the part, and you're the person who can give it to them. After a little chitchat, ask them to read the pages for their character. If you like their first reading, give them a little input on how you see the part and ask them to do it again. Inform them if the part has any special requirement, such as nudity or bungee jumping. That's it. Thank each person for coming and usher the next one in. After meeting about twenty people, you may be tempted to lock yourself in a closet. Resist this temptation and plow ahead.

It would also be advisable to videotape each person that comes in to audition for you. You can then go through these tapes at your own leisure and whittle down the field to the actor you think can do the best job for you and the film. Also, it gives you a chance to see what each actor looks like on screen. Once you have narrowed the field, it's time for the callbacks.

How to Feel at Ease with the Actors

Perhaps the best circumstance you could hope for is to shoot your film in some remote location with no phones and only weekly mail service. Another possibility would be to shoot a prison movie and stay at the prison. The point is that actors are flighty folk, and who needs to worry about the fact that you may wake up one day to find out that your actors have taken the early train home. It is better to be proactive, so you might want to disable the vehicles belonging to the actors if they drove to the set. Pulling the distributor cap is always a good way of preventing premature flight.

A typical distributer cap, 8-cylinder.
Pick a wire, pull it off, then mix it in with the sound cables.

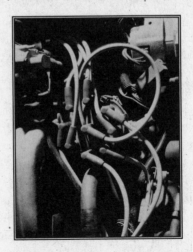

Thespians

Actors who come to you with a classical background in Shake-spearean theater oftentimes spell trouble for filmmakers. They will also spell other words if you ask; they are highly trained. By the way, is it theater or theatre? How come this word has two spellings? Anyhow, when you see a play, there are no close-ups, no medium shots, no zooms or dolly moves. What you see is what you get. The actors and actresses up on the stage use broad motions and big facial expressions so that the cheapskate in the back row—that's right, the guy who smuggled in those Milk Duds—can see what is happening. In film, this definitely doesn't work. We don't want to see a big handshake or a wide-eyed, sorrowful expression magnified a thousand times its normal size. The key word here is *subtlety*. Film has the ability to pick up the smaller nuances in an actor's performance. Tell him or her to tone it down, or *internalize*. That's a good word that might work for you, and it may even make you sound like a director.

Location
Scouting

Now look at your script. If you have done it correctly, it should take place in one location. Well, what is it? Is it the large haunted mansion on the hill, or is it the beach resort, or how about the college campus? Whatever your location du jour (or your location du the coming weeks) is, find it and then get per-mission to wreak havoc—I mean, film there. And remember, whatever you destroy, you must be prepared to replace, and whatever you change, you must be prepared to return to its orig-inal state. The rule is this: You should leave a location looking as if you were never there. The reason is this: A year later, somebody else might need the very location you used for his or her film. Now, if you leave the place a mess, stiff the owner for $1,000, and leave trash around, you can imagine how the guy who owns the location is going to feel about filmmaking and filmmakers. Don't ruin it for the next guy, and leave everything looking the way you found it or better.

Once you have located the perfect location, negotiate with the location's owner for the right to shoot there. What are you going to offer in exchange for the perfect location? How about a credit in the film: "A big credit with your name on it, in a major motion picture." Try to sound excited when you say this. This, by the way, is the first thing that you offer to anybody you want anything from; no exceptions here. It's dirt cheap and makes the person feel good. The further you get away from New York or Los Angeles, the more likely this exchange of location for credit will work. If you are trying to get permission to shoot in a business location, you might offer to prominently display the company's logo or product in a shot; again, get excited about the opportunity you are providing.

So the owner didn't go for it. It's all right to give a security deposit on a location. It's not like you're actually paying for it; if you put everything back, you get your money back. However, this is as far as you should be prepared to go monetarily. Do not pay some slumlord a hundred bucks a day for the use of his broken-down tenement. I would sooner change the script and have my main character live in the Everglades or some other public land that costs nothing to film in. You must be flexible when you are location scouting. Sure, the script may call for a duplex apartment in the middle of summer, but if that beach cottage is available in the middle of winter, well, that might just be the ticket. It only takes a quick rewrite to fit your movie into an available location. As I said before, your script is never actually finished.

Where do you start looking? Well, you start with your relatives, then move on to friends. Friends of relatives and your old college roommate's parents are next. Again, get the word out, and sooner or later that dream location will reveal itself to you.

Once you have negotiated with the location owner, have him or her sign an agreement giving you permission to shoot at that location for the agreed amount of time. The reason for this is simple. People suck. (Just ask Hobbes or Rousseau or Locke; one of those guys proved that people suck.) Mr. Location Owner might decide to call you the night before you are ready to begin filming and tell you he has had a change of heart. While the contract doesn't totally prevent this nauseating scenario, it does lessen the chance.

Once you have decided upon your location, you should read through your script again. Keep the location in mind and make sure that the scene you have written will work at that location. You might find it necessary to tweak a few things to make it work. This is no big deal, and everybody does it. Conversely, sometimes a location will inspire you to add something to your script that you had not thought about.

Video or Film?

Finally. The moment of truth. The defining question. We all love film, there is no doubt about that, but video also has its advantages. I'll give you some pros and cons, but it's up to you to decide.

Film. It looks great but costs a lot. Because of this cost, you are going to have to be very careful about how you cover a scene. Also, if you don't live on either coast, film equipment can be hard to get your hands on. Film requires some specialized personnel who know what they are doing, such as the DP and the camera assistant. In addition, you will need a soundman.

Regardless of what video format you choose, the cost of videotapes coupled with their relatively long running time will allow you to shoot many more takes and angles than film will allow on your budget. In the postproduction area, you will also save a bundle because you can skip the expensive steps of developing and transferring film to videotape. Video equipment is readily available and quite easy to work. On the down side, some crew members will get less excited about a project shot on video. With the actors, it's a toss-up.

So, punk, what's it going to be?

chapter 5

Film equipment and other stuff

C) ongratulations! You have decided to shoot on film; that makes you a filmmaker. Sounds good, doesn't it? Well, now you have yet another decision. If you are not aware of it, there are two 16-mm film formats: The first is standard 16 mm, and the second is called Super 16. The advantage of Super 16 is the film's aspect ratio.

Aspect Ratio

The **aspect ratio** is the ratio of height to width on the screen. Look at your television. Notice it is wider than it is high. The ratio of your television screen's height to width is 1 to 1:33. That means that your screen is one-third wider than it is tall. At the movie theater, there are two aspect ratios that filmmakers employ today. One is called **flat**, a ratio of 1 to 1:85, and then there is **Cinema-scope**, the ratio being 1 to 2:33. These are both available in 35-mm film. Since you are shooting 16 mm, your options are somewhat different.

Regular 16-mm film is in a ratio of 1 to 1:33, just like your television, and if you could be content to have your film shown on TV, then this would be perfect. Alas, you aspire for more. So here is the rub: When you blow up your film to 35 mm, the lab is going to need to crop the top and bottom of the image to make it fit into the wider 35-mm frame. Keeping this in mind, we want to make sure that nothing crucial to the story sits at the very bottom or top of the frame, because when your film is blown up to 35 mm, this area will be lost. Another option is to shoot on Super 16 film. The aspect ratio of this format is 1 to 1:66; this falls exactly in between the ratio of standard 16 mm and 35 mm. The net result is that less area at the top or the bottom will have to be cropped, therefore reducing the grain when you blow your film up to 35 mm. This, however, is not the only benefit of Super 16. To get this wider aspect ratio, Super 16 uses the area on the right side of the film-strip that used to contain sprocket holes. Instead, this second strip of sprocket holes is deleted and emulsion covers this area all the way to the film's edge. By offsetting the lens and widening the gate inside the camera, you expose an image onto this area. This 16-mm film stock is known as **single perf** because the perforations or sprocket holes only run down one side of the film.

Equipment

What equipment do you need to make a feature-length film, and how are you going to get it? You could steal it. This is very risky, but the publicity would be great. Imagine the interviews. You would be on the cover of *Premiere* magazine holding up a Slim Jim and a crowbar yelling, "Who needs credit cards!?!"

OK, snap out of it. Enough of filmmaker fantasy number one;

we all know this one by heart, anyhow. It goes like this. Your feature-film debut goes on to win the Sundance Film Festival. Shortly afterward, your picture graces the cover of every indie film rag and the "Arts and Leisure" section of the Sunday *New York Times*. From there, you move to Hollywood, buy a huge house and a fancy car, and get hooked on heroin. OK, the last part is optional. But all this is going to have to wait, because before you can make a film, you need a couple of essential pieces of equipment.

You need a Nagra reel-to-reel tape recorder or a DAT (digital audiotape) field recorder. Shooting in 16 mm, chances are you will never get further than video distribution. However, you still have the possibility of going for blowup to 35 mm if lightning strikes. You all know what a camera is, but what the hell is a Nagra? You have seen one before; you just don't know it. Think back to any police story when the guys are in the stakeout van recording their prime suspect's conversations. Yes, that reel-to-reel tape recorder they are using is a piece of film equipment called a Nagra.

While the Nagra is very reliable and now quite cheap to rent, the trend with soundmen today is the DAT (digital audiotape) recorder. The DAT records digitally, so the quality is quite high and the prices are reasonable for rental. You will need a DAT recorder with time code. Time code is the DAT's internal clock, much like the crystal in the Nagra.

DAT recorders are not that expensive, and the convenience and audio quality will more than make up for the cost. If this option is available to you, I recommend it highly.

In summation:

Nagra, the older workhorse, is cheaper to rent and records on open-reel tapes.

DAT, the new technology, is moderately priced and records on nice, neat cassettes.

What else do you need? Plenty.

Don't Leave Home
Without It

Here is a list of equipment that is absolutely necessary in order to
make a motion picture:

1. A 16-mm camera with crystal sync
2. A reel-to-reel tape recorder with crystal or a DAT recorder
   with time code
3. A tripod with a fluid head
4. Microphones and assorted sound cables
5. Batteries for the camera
6. A slate and gaffer's tape

Would Be Nice

The following items would be nice to have while shooting your
film:

1. A small lighting package
2. A wheelchair or a doorway dolly
3. C-stands and flags (basic grip equipment)

Money to Burn

You'll probably only be able to afford these items if you have
money to burn:

1. A grip truck
2. A track dolly and miles of track
3. HMI lighting

Sound Equipment

If you want to know how a DAT recorder works, go take a course in electronics at your local trade school. For your purposes, all we need to know is this: A sound recorder takes an audio input from a microphone and encodes it and records it on a magnetic medium for playback later.

Along with your Nagra or DAT recorder, you are going to need a few other items. For starters, a good quality **microphone** is important. Mikes come in many varieties with some very confusing pickup patterns and characteristics. You might come across terms like *cardioid* or *hypercardioid* or *omnidirectional*. Well, forget all that junk. The longer the mike, the smaller its pickup pattern, or the more directional it is. One good, long mike should do you just fine. You are going to put this mike in what's called a **shock mount,** a little contraption that is crisscrossed with rubber bands into which the mike slips. You will then put this at the end of a very expensive broomstick with a rubber grip called a **boom.** Take a sound cable and connect it to the back of the mike and run it into the mike input on your Nagra or DAT recorder. You are now ready to record sound.

An even better solution would be to run all your sound cables into a mixer. Then the soundperson can set the appropriate level for each microphone before the audio signal reaches the DAT recorder.

The Camera

For those who have grown up in the video age, the **motion-picture camera** may be a rather daunting piece of technology. Video cameras have twenty to thirty switches, buttons, doodads, and an instruction manual that you need a Ph.D. to understand. Motion-picture cameras have only one switch: on and off. If you have a better camera, it might have a dial for variable speed, but this is a luxury you cannot afford. The faster the camera, the more film it uses and the poorer you become.

The idea here is to get the cheapest 16-mm camera you can find that has crystal sync. The crystal is a piece of quartz that regulates the flow of electricity, keeping the camera and the DAT recorder running at the same speed. Today, there are several 16-mm cameras one can choose from. There is the ARRI SR series, the most modern being the ARRI SR3 and the oldest being the plain-old ARRI SR. There is also the Aaton, and to a lesser extent, Panavision. I would call these the first tier of 16-mm cameras, meaning that they're more expensive to rent but fine pieces of machinery that will give you good performance.

However, if you opt for a camera that's less in demand, you will probably get a better rental price. Eclair—and I'm talking about the camera, not the pastry—is a good choice for an older-generation camera that might be less demanding on your pocketbook.

? POP QUIZ: Which is the eclair camera, photo A or photo B?

Isn't it just like the French to name a camera after their favorite creme-filled dessert? Both the NPR and the ACL are made by Eclair and are excellent cameras. Also, check into Aatons and Movie Cams. You should be able to rent these for considerably less than the ARRI SR. The ARRI SR series are the most prevalent 16-mm cameras used today. The SR1 and SR2 are very similar and should be cheaper to rent than the newer SR3. If money is tight, why not use an older generation of ARRI cameras? The 16 BL is a very sturdy workhorse. Shop around, get the best prices, and remember: all cameras are basically the same. They have a mechanical device that moves the film past the lens, stopping it for a brief moment, exposing it to light, and then moving it away. A good camera will keep the film steady when the shutter is open. This is known as **registration**. Image quality is really dependent on the lens you use in front of the camera. So if it works and the price is right, by all means go for it.

One final word on the camera: It has to be quiet. Even if the camera can hold sync, it will be of no use to you if it's louder than a sewing machine. So before you rent a camera, have the guy who is renting it pop on a magazine, preferably with a dummy load of film in it (yes, they make different amounts of noise with and without film), and give a listen.

The Lens

The lens you choose for your camera will dictate the sharpness of your image. To those with more sensitive eyes, lenses actually have color characteristics as well. However, for our purposes, sharpness is a top priority. Lenses come in two general categories: **prime** and **zoom**.

Prime lenses have a fixed focal length. Their big advantage is that they are sharper than zoom lenses and also have a lower f-stop. That means they are a much better choice than a zoom for a low-light interior scene.

Before you get too excited and decide to shoot your feature film with a set of primes, let's look at the realities of working with a set of these lenses. Yup, a set. Because they have a fixed focal length you need a wide angle, about a 10 mm, and a couple of midrange lenses, usually a 16, a 25, and a 50. And on the telephoto end, maybe a 75. Now that you have a case of lenses, pop it open. Grab one and throw it on the camera and see what happens.

Say you chose a 50-mm prime lens, look through the camera, and decide you want to be closer to the subject. You now have two choices. You can pick up the camera and physically move it closer to the subject, or you can change to a 75-mm prime. A set of prime lenses will give you a much sharper image than a zoom lens. A prime lens is any lens that has a set focal length. However, a zoom will make your life a whole lot easier. The most popular zoom lens is the Angenoux 12–120 mm. Other available zooms are the 10–150 mm, which will give you a slightly wider angle, or the 9.5–57 mm, which is even wider. Both of these lenses are also made by Angenoux. There is also a 10–100 made by Cooke and a 7–63 mm made by Canon. These two more modern lenses will cost you a little more money, but they both give you a relatively wide-angle zoom and are very sharp.

How can you tell if the lens is any good? A lens is a precision instrument and it should feel like one. All of its movements should be smooth and precise. Turn the barrel; crunchy noises or squeaks are warning signs. Also, watch out for jumpy movements and scratched elements. If the lens looks abused, chances are that it has been and you should try to get another.

F-STOPS AND T-STOPS
F-stops are the numbers on your lens that determine how much light will pass through the barrel striking the film.

The **f-stop** is a purely mathematical equation that takes into account the lens's focal length and diameter. The diameter can be changed by adjusting the aperture. The larger the aperture, the more light it is letting through the lens. In the motion-picture industry, we use something known as T-stops.

A **T-stop** also takes into account the light that is lost as it travels through a lens, reflecting off its various elements. In essence, a T-stop is a more exact f-stop. On your lens, there are going to be two sets of numbers: f-stops and T-stops. They are going to be exactly identical except for the lowest number on the scale. The one with the lower number is the f-stop scale; the one with higher number is the T-stop scale. The guy in between second and third is the shortstop. Use T-stops—especially when traveling in Boston.

Now, if film technicians are so finicky about f-stops and T-stops, how come they read their light meters at 1/50 of a second instead of 1/48 of a second? Well, write a letter and find out. A good place to send it would be American Cinematographer, c/o ASK ASC, P.O. Box 2230, Hollywood, CA 90028. They might answer your question in an issue of the magazine they publish. Any other questions you have should also be addressed to the above address. Just be willing to accept the fact that your questions may never get answered.

DEPTH OF FIELD

Have you ever noticed that when you take a picture outside with a wide-angle lens everything seems to be in sharp focus? Conversely, that great shot you rushed off at your sister's wedding, the one in the chapel that she counted on you to get as she walked in with the candle in her hand . . . well, in that picture, everything including your sister is out of focus, even though you swore you had focused on the candle. After all, she was holding the candle five inches in front of her, so why the hell is she out of focus—and for that matter, not talking to you?

These are examples of **depth of field.** Depth of field refers to the area in the frame that will appear to be in focus. When you have very little depth of field, most things will be out of focus— like your sister. When you have a lot of depth of field, everything will be in focus.

Depth of field is a function of two things: the size (in millimeters) of the lens you are using and the T-stop the lens is set at. The wider the angle of the lens, the more depth of field you will have, regardless of the T-stop. So a 16-mm lens has more depth of field, while a 200 mm will have less. The other factor that affects depth of field is your lens's aperture opening, or T-stop, if you are shooting all the way open. That mean the little iris inside the lens is open as far as it can go, thus permitting the maximum amount of light to pass through the lens. This is usually somewhere around a T-2; with that setting, you will have substantially less depth of field than if you were shooting at T-16. By combining different focal length lenses and changing the amount of light reaching the lenses either through lighting or with filters, you can manipulate the depth of field for your creative purposes. Just keep in mind that when you have a very small depth of field, focus becomes very critical—and nothing is worse than a crucial shot that is out of focus. For the beginner, I would suggest that you shoot with wider lenses—especially at night, when you can't get a lot of light on the subject.

Sound Equipment

Sound is the most overlooked aspect of independent filmmaking. It is also the one that will cost you the most money to fix later, so let's take a moment to make sure that you do it right the first time.

If you are outside, your major enemies are going to be wind and airplanes. Short of buying a Stinger missile from Saddam Hussein, there really is nothing you can do about an airplane flying overhead. Just let the plane go by and then resume shooting. As far as the wind is concerned, there are many things that you can do to keep recording quality sound.

If you shoot outside, you will need a **windscreen,** a gray, screenlike thing that looks like a hollow salami. Place it over the microphone to prevent the wind from hitting it and destroying your sound. If it gets really windy, you can cover this with a furry thing that looks like a Muppet condom. Trust me, you'll know it when you see it.

WIRELESS MICROPHONES

A **wireless microphone** can be worn by an actor under his or her clothing. You can clip a miniature microphone somewhere close to the actor's mouth, hidden under their clothing. For some reason, all soundpeople despise these clip-on microphones, but they usually get a very clear recording. Also, because they are so close to the actors, there is usually a minimal amount of background noise even if you are in a bad environment. The argument goes as follows. You are rushing to get a shot and the soundman keeps on moving his microphone into the frame as he attempts to get it as close as possible to the actor. The sun is going down, so you say screw the boom, just clip a wireless on. Now, for some reason, all soundpeople take great offense at this suggestion, as if you were challenging their very manhood. I don't know if it has something to do with holding the boom or what, but trust me, the very next thing you are going to hear is "It doesn't sound right if we use the wireless." Remember, the sun is going down. Be strong and respond, "Just clip the thing on, and let's get rolling."

HEADPHONES

When you record sound, it is a good idea to wear **headphones.** This will allow you to listen to the direct output of what the DAT is actually recording. That way you can be sure that your levels are correct. You also will be able to make sure you are actually recording what you are hearing. Do yourself a favor and don't use those little headphones that you stole during your last flight home on JetBlue. It's important that you can hear your sound clearly without a lot of outside interference. You should get headphones that cover your ears completely so you can be sure that the sound you are hearing is coming through the microphone and being recorded on the soundtrack, not coming from the car idling loudly behind you fifty feet away from the microphone and will be of no consequence to your soundtrack.

CABLES

Professional sound cables are essential for recording quality sound. These are not the cables that you use to hook up your home stereo system. Just in case you were wondering, those are called RCA cables. They have the little prong that looks like a penis in the middle of a metal ring. (However, the penis is the perfect size for the receptor, so who is to say that it is little?) Professional sound cables are known as XLR cables. They have a metal circle about half an inch in diameter, and inside that are three pins. This is known as a male connector because of the three sets of pins (this correlates perfectly with the male anatomy, because you and I know that many men have three penises). Want to guess what the other end of the cable is called, the one that has three holes? Yup, the female connector. The microphone connects to this end and then the male end is plugged into the sound recorder or a mixer that feeds the sound recorder. A good thing to remember is that sound cables often fail. Don't ask why. It just happens, so make sure you have a couple spares on hand.

Fluid Head

A tripod with a fluid head is also essential. A **fluid head** will smooth out your tilts and pans. It works by displacing fluid in a matrix of electromagnetically charged ectoplasm. When you pan or tilt, you produce an excess of neutrons that combine with the free-floating electrons, thereby creating a dampening effect.

All of the above is a lie. I have no idea how it works, it just does. Really, all you need to know is that you need a fluid head. Nobody is going to ask you to take it apart or refill it when you're done.

Light Meter

In order to tell how much light is present, you must acquaint yourself with a little gizmo known as the **light meter.** This device will tell you at what f-stop (or lens opening) you will be shooting the scene. I like the Minolta Auto Meter III. (No, they are not paying me a dime to mention their name, but I would gladly accept payment.) You just hold it up to the subject and press the button on the side. The little digital display on the front will tell you the proper exposure.

Better yet, this light meter can also sometimes pass as a Geiger counter. Try it, it's fun. The next time you are riding in an elevator, pull it out and press the button. Then discuss with your companion how many rads of radiation this building is leaking because it was built on an old fuel dump containing PCBs.

The only things you need to know about setting up your light meter are the ASA of the film and the speed at which your camera will be running. If you are shooting a scene with sound, your camera speed is 1/48 of a second, which is rounded off to 1/50 of a second. The Exposure Index (EI) of your film stock is printed on the can it comes in. Input these two numbers into your light meter according to the instructions. Your meter might have the letters EV on it somewhere, or maybe the letters DIN. But as an American filmmaker, you will want nothing to do with either of these. Yes, these are from the makers of the metric system—our friends across the ocean who do everything a little differently. Now, go to your fridge and look at your milk container. What is it measured in? Ah, good old American quarts! Give it a sniff, and if it's curdled, toss it down the drain. If not, take a victory sip. Yes, you are still buying your milk in quarts, so you will still be reading your light meter in f-stops and inputting your film speed as an ASA value, either ISO or EI, but never DIN.

OK, your light meter has been set up. Take a meter reading. Somewhere on the meter there will be a little white ball. This ball represents a human face, albeit a very dull person. You hold this ball up to the face of the person you are lighting. Pointing the ball toward the camera, press the button.

The meter will now show you a number representing the total amount of light that is penetrating the ball and reaching the light-sensitive chip hidden behind. You will then transfer this number to the lens, and the subject you have metered should be exposed properly on film.

Sounds easy, doesn't it? Well, here is the problem. Anybody can expose film properly, but what sets a great director of photography apart from the rest of the pack is his or her ability to use these numbers and translate them into an exact look by adding and subtracting lights to various areas on the set to achieve the desired effect.

Lighting

If you are shooting indoors, you are going to need lights. The name of the game in lighting a scene effectively is called **control**. This means the ability to have light where you want it and, equally important, the ability to have darkness or shadow where you want them as well. In order to achieve these goals, the DP has many tools available to him or her. For the purposes of our low-budget film, let's take a look at the lights that will be of the most use while not breaking the bank.

PHOTOFLOODS

The cheapest lights are called **photofloods**. These lightbulbs are built to scale for the hands of basketball players. Other people holding one will make the bulb look ridiculously large. You can buy photofloods at your local photo emporium. These jumbo bulbs are color corrected to 3,200 and 5,500 degrees Kelvin. You just screw these guys into an available socket and you're ready to shoot. These babies get real hot, so watch out. Now, this is not a very good way to light a scene, but it is cheap.

FRESNELS

You're making a movie, and by God, you want those big lights you saw on the street the other day. The most useful light is called a **fresnel,** which gets its name from the ridged lens that covers the opening that the light passes through. This lens evens out the light. Fresnels come in various sizes, ranging from two hundred watts to twelve thousand watts. In order to plug a light into a socket that you recognize, the largest lamp you can use is two thousand watts, or a 2K for short. The sockets in your wall are called Edison, just like the guy who invented the lightbulb. Any light above two thousand watts will have a plug at the end that will not fit into the wall socket, no matter how much force you apply, because it is shaped differently.

The fresnel is the classic movie light you have seen countless times. If you go into the novelty shop at Universal Studios, this is the light that the miniature desktop movie light complete with studio logo is modeled after. The bulb inside this light is on a track that is connected to a knob on the outside of the unit. By turning this knob, you can change the position of the bulb and the reflector that travels along with it inside the light. When the bulb is moved all the way forward, the light is at **full flood;** this means the light will cover a large area with equal intensity. Conversely, when the bulb is all the way to the rear of the unit, it will be in **full spot.** The light's intensity will be greater while covering a smaller area.

OPEN-FACE LIGHTS

The open-face light is another common type of lighting device. The most common sizes for this unit are 650, 1,000 and 2,000 watts. Just as the name implies, these lights have an open face. There is nothing between the bulb and, well, you. These lights are usually lightweight, so they are great when you need a unit you can hang from a rafter or attach to a clamp atop some molding. They are also good as a bounce light. And when things get really bad and you forget to pay your oil bill, you can also use them as a space heater. They throw off a lot of heat.

PAR LIGHTS

The key aspect of this type of light is the shape of the reflector behind the bulb. Like a car headlight, it is shaped like a parabola. The result is these units put out an enormous amount of concentrated light. They are great for bouncing light off a wall or a white card if you want to fill a location with ambient light. Pars also have a good throw, so if you want to light a building across the street, this would be the unit of choice.

HMIs

These lights produce about three times the amount of illumination per watt than your ordinary tungsten unit. They are color balanced for daylight, which means they emit a bluish light. These lights are more expensive than their tungsten cousins. HMI lights use a combination of metals in the bulb that cause them to burn at the proper color temperature that emulates daylight. (Just in case someone asks, HMI stands for Hydrargyum Medium Arc-Length Iodide. You can amaze your friends and win many bets with this otherwise useless knowledge.)

The advantage of using an HMI is this: Since the light is balanced toward the blue end of the spectrum, it matches the color temperatures one will encounter when shooting outside. If you are shooting outdoors, or if you have a location that has many big windows and you need to add a little supplemental lighting, HMI are perfect because there is no need to filter either the camera or the windows to make the color temperature of all the light sources match up. The second big advantage of HMIs is light output. For a comparable wattage in another light, an HMI puts out three to four times as much light. That means a twelve-hundred-watt HMI light puts out as much light as a five-thousand-watt tungsten light. That is really cool because nothing attracts attention more than a really bright light.

CHINA BALLS

Perhaps one of the most useful lights for the independent production is the **china ball,** or paper globe. (By the way, now would be a good time to make a reservation at your favorite Chinese restaurant. Take the wife or girlfriend out because by now she is probably totally fed up with your whole filmmaking obsession.) The china ball produces a nice soft light and is lightweight. In fact, it's so light that you can usually just have your gaffer tape them directly to the ceiling. This makes them easy to hang. Along with the china ball, you are going to need some of those brown or white twelve-foot extension cords. You will also tape these to the ceiling and then run the wire down a wall that will not be filmed and plug it in. It's that easy. You can control the light by draping duvetyn around the area you don't want light to escape from.

Did you make your reservation at the Garden Wok yet? Good, because tonight as you eat the Peking duck and that flaky fish that they leave the eyeballs on you are going to acquire some grade-A film-lighting equipment. First, ask to be seated on the patio, the place where these globes are usually strung. Remember, you want the white ones, not the red ones—and definitely not the ones shaped like a paper fish. After the meal—and I mean a full meal that includes Pu Pu platter and green tea ice cream—you should be able to walk away with at least three of these paper globes.

If your girlfriend stops you, then I suggest going to IKEA. She will once again love you, and you will be able to buy your china balls in various sizes for about five bucks a pop (if you don't factor in all the collapsible furniture your S.O. picks up along the way as you creep through the maze of Swedish furniture). If you are single, this is a good place to pick up girls and lure them into participating in your film.

Plugging It In

When you arrive on your set, you should be equipped with some basic hardware that will make your life a whole lot easier. Next to the camera, the most important item is that little doodad that converts a three-pronged plug into a two-pronged plug. Bring plenty of these, because they tend to disappear often.

Here's another useful item. It's one of those things that you screw into a light socket that converts it into a plug. Extension cords are also a necessary item, and I don't mean those little thin brown ones with the three plugs at the end and that weird, twisty thing. You are going to need something a little more heavy-duty made from 14- or 16-gauge wire. The smaller the number, the thicker the wire is inside the extension cord. The thicker the wire, the more current it can carry. The more current it can carry, the longer you can run it without overheating it and burning it out. You can usually pick these guys up at construction sights at about 2 A.M. If worse comes to worst, go to your local home improvement center. (Once again, I receive nothing from these people. I just like hanging out in that kind of store. It makes anyone feel like an able carpenter. Just try going in there without pricing lumber.) Now, remember that these mega home improvement stores have very liberal return policies, so we are going to slip these guys carefully out of their wrappers and then save the packaging and receipts in a closet somewhere so we can return the cords later on.

Fuses

The first thing you should do at your location is find the fuse box. Pull the sucker open and take a look. If it is filled with ten-amp fuses, your life has just been made a little harder. If pennies have been substituted for fuses, you are going to fry the wiring, burn down your location, and be arrested for arson. If the box contains twenty-amp fuses things are OK. Anything above twenty amps and you should give the owner a big hug. If the box is equipped with old screw-in fuses instead of circuit breakers, make sure you pick up some spares at the hardware store.

Ten amps is the amount of electricity a thousand-watt lamp will pull through a line. (Actually it's 8.3 amps, but the idea here is not to blow fuses, so we are rounding upward.) What this means for you is that on a ten-amp circuit you can plug in up to a thousand watts of lighting equipment. One fuse may be connected to four sockets, but the total draw from all four cannot be over a thousand watts.

You will usually find larger amounts of electricity in kitchens, bathrooms, and rooms with air conditioners.

HINT: **Opposing walls are usually on the same circuit.**

HINT: **If you're not sure about something electrical, have somebody else touch it first.**

HINT: **If the plug dangling from the movie light looks like something from the space shuttle, do not try and force it into an outlet.**

The Tie-In

A tie-in is something your gaffer or electrician will need to be familiar with if you must use a light rated at more than two thousand watts. I'm going to tell you what a tie-in is, but don't even think of attempting it from the description in this book. This is an operation that can *kill* you if it is not performed properly. The idea is this: Since you can't get enough electricity from any outlet in the house to power up the lights, you have to go directly to the source. That's right—the electrical panel. First, pop the panel off, then connect cables to the main lines that feed the panel from the street. These cables look like car jumper cables, only instead of two wires there are three, the third being for a ground. So one cable goes to the feed, the next to the earth wire, and the third to the ground. The other side of these cables will be connected to your own electrical distribution box. From this box, you will get your power and connect your feeder cables.

The other essential element of the tie-in is a two-by-four.

While the first electrician attaches the cables to the box, the second stands ready with the two-by-four. If by chance the guy connecting the cables makes a mistake and manages to channel the electric current through his body, the man with the two-by-four is there to swat him away from the box, thereby breaking the circuit that he has become part of and hopefully saving his life.

Grip Equipment

Grip equipment is usually available from the same location that rented you your lighting supplies. Think of grip equipment as outrageously priced hardware. One example of a useful grip item is a flag. Flags are black squares of cloth on wire frames. If you built them yourself, it would cost a couple of bucks. But who would want to do this when you can rent them for $10 a day? Flags are used to block light so it doesn't hit an undesired area on the set. Nets are similar to flags; they have the same construction, but instead of black cloth they have a fine mesh strung across the frame. The result is that they only block out a portion of the light. Flags come in two varieties, a double or a single; they have a colored piping that runs around their border so you can tell them apart. White piping is for singles and red piping is for doubles. When placed in front of a light source, a double will take down the amount of light reaching the intended subject by one f-stop. A single will drop the light down by one-half an f-stop.

Clamps, Gobos, C-Stands, and Whatnot

Other useful items are furniture clamps for hanging lights, and C-stands for flying flags and nets. A C-stand looks like a light stand that got too close to the nuclear power plant. It has three short, stubby legs that swing out. You can usually recognize one by the sticker that reads "Century Stand" affixed to it. Fixed atop a C-stand you will find something called a gobo and another stick of metal called the arm. The **gobo** is a circle about four inches in diameter with a knob on one side. On the other side, you'll see a fitting that will slip onto the stud on top of the C-stand. Around the circumference of the circle you will find three holes of varying diameters. The holes are opened by loosening the knuckle, allowing you to slide objects into them. You can then tighten the knuckle, holding the object tight in the gobo's grip.

Other essential grip equipment includes an apple box, which is a wooden box about nine inches high, a foot wide, and two feet long. You also need various clamps, including studded C-clamps, spring clamps, scissors clamps, maffers, and furniture clamps. The clamps are used to hang lights above doorways or from the ceiling or any other place you can't have a light stand present.

Steadicam

We have all seen those beautiful gliding shots produced by the Steadicam. If you can afford it, by all means get one for a couple of days. But remember: Don't trust an owner/operator unless he has a middle name. For example, in colonial days John Paul Jones would have made an excellent Steadicam operator while George Washington would not. A two-name owner operator is immediately suspect in my book. *Beware!* An exception to this rule is anyone with two names followed by Jr.; a Jr. is OK. That person is most likely part of a family of Steadicam operators and has it in his blood.

Wheelchair

I'm glad you have returned to your senses. Sure, the Steadicam would have been nice; and no, the Steadicam Jr. will not work in its place. But there is a tool waiting at the local drugstore that should fill in nicely. Yes, the wheelchair. Just plop your operator into the seat, and you two can produce beautiful gliding shots as long as you have a smooth surface to roll on. But watch those stops and starts—those front wheels tend to jerk you around a little.

Gels

Gels are those colorful sheets of plastic that you see in front of lights. Although they look like the stuff that comes wrapped around a gift basket, they are much different. For starters, they are fire retardant, so when the hot lights hit them they will not spontaneously combust. The second and perhaps most important feature is that they are manufactured to very strict tolerances, so when you place a gel in front of a light, you know how it will affect the light's color temperature and light output.

There are two basic gels with which you should familiarize yourself: the **full blue** and the **CTO**. The full blue will change the temperature of tungsten light to that of daylight. The CTO gel will change the temperature of a daylight-balanced light to tungsten. It's that easy. By the way, remember those clothespins you stole from your mother? You will be using those to connect the gels to the lights. Both blue and CTO gels come in fractions ranging from ⅛ to one full f-stop.

There are a few other gels you should familiarize yourself with. Please take a look at the list that follows.

Minus green
Plus green
Neutral density (or ND) 0.3–1.2
Opal diffusion
216 diffusion

These are the most common gels you will encounter. You should call up a motion-picture lighting store, such as Barbizon, and request gel swatch books from both Rosco and Lee, the two largest manufacturers of gels.

Grand Larceny

So where are you going to get all this stuff from if you're not going to steal it? First, ask everybody you know if they have any of this stuff laying around in their attic. If that doesn't work, you could try taking some classes at a local university that has a program in film. Sign out the equipment to shoot your class project and at the same time shoot your feature film. When you return the equipment late, blame it on the uncooperative weather. As an absolute last resort, well, you might actually have to rent the equipment. That's right, spend money.

Rentals

HINT: **Make friends with guys at the rental house; go to a smaller company, where you can get to know the guy in charge.**

All else has failed and we are going to rent the equipment needed. How do we do it?

First, let's schedule our shoot for nine days starting on a Saturday and ending the following Sunday. Most equipment rental houses do not charge for weekends. Also, most charge a weekly rate that is equal to three times the daily rate. Call your local rental house and arrange to pick up your equipment late on a Friday. Tell the clerk or manager that you are shooting the sunrise on the following Monday morning; this way, they will not be tempted to charge you for the weekend. Also mention that you will be using the equipment until very late on Friday. They will then inform you that the equipment must be returned first thing Monday morning or they will have to charge you for an extra day. Smile and tell them you will have the equipment back. Now, here is the good part. You have scheduled it so that the Monday when the equipment is due back happens to be a national holiday. Good ones to plan around are Memorial Day and Labor Day. These two always hit on Mondays. Guess what? You just got an additional day for free. If everything works properly you will get ten days for the price of three!

Insurance

Film equipment is expensive. You could go to your local hardware store and buy a broomstick for about three bucks. If you take this same broomstick and place a rubber grip on the bottom and paint it jet black and stencil the word *boom* on it, well, *presto!* You could sell it for $300! A 16-mm camera costs anywhere from $10,000 to $40,000. Do you think a rental company is just going to let you throw that baby into your trunk without some type of guarantee? No way. It's going to want a certificate of insurance naming it as the loss-payee. In English, that means that when you lose the camera, they get the money.

You have two options when it comes to insurance. (No, your homeowner's policy will not work.) First, you can call one of the companies that specializes in selling insurance to film companies. They will ask you how much coverage you will need over how many days. Ask for $100,000 over the duration of the shoot. Then they will give you a quote. They will probably try and sell you all other kinds of insurance with names like *negative insurance*. This type of insurance covers any damage that may happen to your negative.

Just stick with what you need. Who needs the extra expense and headache of dealing with an insurance company for any of these fringe insurance items? It's hard enough to make heads or tails out of your car insurance.

An easier way to obtain insurance is to rent from an equipment house that will sell you coverage of its own. For a premium that falls in between 10 and 20 percent of your rental fee, the house will cover you with its own insurance. Normally, there will be a hefty deductible in the $1,000 range.

Just plan on not losing any cameras down the Colorado River and everything will be fine.

How to Keep Your Camera in New York City

You are walking back to your car, camera in hand, and notice your car is leaning heavily in front. As you approach your car, you see the front tire is flat. Alas, a Good Samaritan is there to tell you about your flat tire. You get busy with the jack and the spare while all the time this guy is talking to you, kind of blocking you with his body, maybe even helping you with the odd lug nut. When you go to thank him, he is gone. You go to return the jack to the trunk and then you notice your camera is gone, too. Well, this is the basic scam that these operatives have developed to separate you from your camera equipment. Other variations on the theme are the stranger pointing out the $20 bill on the sidewalk and the man from Ethiopia who has come to pick up his inheritance. I didn't stick around long enough to see how the latter one played out, but it sure seemed interesting. The thing to keep in mind is this: Be very wary of anybody who approaches you when you are carrying a camera down the street. The best tactic is to be a little rude and don't get caught up in any of those street theater performances when you have film equipment with you.

Money Talks

Most businesses associated with the film industry are located in the back rooms of industrial-type buildings, the kind that have long been abandoned by Fortune 500 companies. Even more important for you, most do not have cash boxes or anything that remotely resembles a cash register. Don't ever expect to get the proper change back, especially when you hand over a large bill at one of these locations. Change for the bus is definitely out of the question.

Most companies catering to the film industry are accustomed to accepting company checks, and now most will accept credit cards, too. For these forms of payment, you will get the standard quoted price know as the **rate card.** Why? Because this is the price that is printed on the rate card. The most important thing to know about the rate card is that nobody pays the price on the rate card. At the very least, you can ask if that is the best price, and instantly you will probably get 10 percent off the rate card. However, the discounts get deeper and the bargaining more intense when you pull out a wad of cash. You might think you are bargaining for a rug in the open-air markets of Kashmir. (It will smell about the same.) At the absolute least, you should be able to get sales tax off by waving some greenbacks around. But you should be able to get more.

Make an offer and see what happens. The worst they can say is no. If they do say no, then walk out. Thank them for their time and go for the door. If they call you back, you have a deal, so whip out the cash. Where does this cash go? Well, chances are they will fold it up and stuff it deep into their front pocket, so deep that Uncle Sam will never reach it. So don't be afraid to offer smaller amounts of cash, and by all means shop around. Look for the smaller, seedier supply places; the ones tucked away far from sunlight and close to the boiler room. Those establishments will most likely be easily swayed by cash waving. Larger places such as established labs and postproduction facilities (posthouses) will not be as swayed by the almighty dollar, unless they are in bankruptcy.

Another good idea is to dress poor. Wear old clothing a couple of sizes too small and pay with old, crinkled-up bills. If they feel sorry for you, they might come down a little on the price. If you want to get the feel for one of these places, go to Rafik. It's in New York City on Broadway between Twelfth and Thirteenth Streets. The slanted stairs that lead to this second-floor establishment are truly a treat. Once you have safely navigated yourself to the entrance, you will be served by a film hippie who, more often than not, will make a mistake while adding up your bill. If it's not in your favor, point out the error; if it is in your favor, smile and try not to break your neck while running down the stairs.

"Will You Take a Personal Check?"

Don't count on it. Filmmaking is a risky business, and nobody knows it better than the film labs. The last thing they want to do is take a personal check from somebody they have never done business with before. Unfortunately, you are not the first person to try to make a film for almost no money, and although the process is new to you, the labs have seen it all before. Since only approximately one film in a hundred is successful, that leaves the film labs with ninety-nine broke filmmakers trying to pass off a bad check. Rather than take bogus paper notes, the labs will hang on to your film negative. They have vaults full of unclaimed film from bankrupt production companies. You are not the first to try to scam them, and you will not be the last.

Negotiations

As you move forward with this film, you will be negotiating with two basic groups. The first group is people that you want things from for free or next to free. The second group is people to whom you will actually be paying money in exchange for goods or services.

We already know that when dealing with the first group, your best offer is going to be a credit in the film. When dealing with people you are actually paying, you might have a little more leeway in you negotiations. The best tactic is what I call the "I will have to get back to you" method. It goes something like this: Call up the labs or equipment houses or individuals that you are going to deal with. Talk at length about your job and then ask for a price quote. Once they give you the price, thank them, leave them your phone number, and tell them you will get back to them. Then do nothing. Wait and wait and wait. You see, the hungry people will call you back, and once somebody calls you back you can use that fact to leverage yourself a much better price. In order for this system to work, you must call multiple vendors for each service or position you wish to fill. You should also note that the lowest bidder is not always the best person for you. You have to balance an overriding, inbred American desire to get a great deal with the reality that if the person or facility cannot deliver the goods, you are going to be screwed.

Deferred Pay

Deferring pay is a negotiating tool that works best with actors and crew members. So, you're having a little trouble convincing actors to work for free. Offer them some money. Tell them you will give them $500 a day, deferred. Yes, the key word here is *deferred*. I will spell it out phonetically. It is pronounced like this: U-WILL-NEVER-SEE-A-STINKEN-CENT.

Deferred pay works like this: After you pay all the expenses associated with production—lab costs, equipment rentals, loan sharks, your Visa bill, and any others costs you can make up—you then pay all those with whom you have a deferred-pay deal. Because deferred pay only kicks in after the film has made its money back, and because the filmmaker controls who gets paid, you never have to pay anyone because you can claim that the film didn't make money. I think every professional has probably worked on a deferred-pay project at one time or another in his or her career. The problem is that most of these people have never actually seen a deferred payment. I say this so you can prepare yourself for the quick dismissals and turns downs this avenue is sure to produce. On the other hand, people who are relatively new to the business might be willing to try out deferred pay if they trust you. It, of course, will be the last time they ever trust you.

Send the Girl In (or Guy)

If you are fortunate to have a pretty girl in your group, you may qualify for special treatment, discounts, gift items, and unadvertised perks. Girls are rare in the film industry; even rarer are pretty heterosexual girls (PHGs for short). PHG could also stand for pretty homosexual girl, and I want to make it very clear that this technique will work equally well for both groups regardless of their sexual preference.

When an above-average PHG, type one or type two, enters a film lab or an equipment rental house, she will immediately be helped. I once had the pleasure of going to a certain lab that I won't name (which was located in New York City and had a name made up of three capital letters that started with T and ended with C and now happens to be no longer in business) with a member of the female gender. Upon entering the door, no less than three men immediately greeted her by name. A small fight ensued over who would have the privilege of handing her the box containing her film dailies. In short, if you know a good-looking girl, she may be entitled to some unwritten discounts at the film lab. This type of discount is not just limited to women and heterosexuals. The secret is to find out the counter person's sexual preference and then send in the appropriate member of the crew whose physical and sexual attributes most closely align to secure the most favorable discount. Is it just a coincidence that the men who work at the lab look remarkably similar to the men who patronize your local strip bar? But ask yourself: Why are they familiar from those establishments? Because you go there, too. Of course, your excuse is that you are scouting a location.

Try stretching the boundaries. Have your girlfriend dress on the slutty side; it can't hurt. Who knows, if these guys get dizzy enough they may forget about the money you owe them, and your girlfriend might emerge with enough cash for a slice of pizza.

Lighting
Strategies

Good taste has a lot to do with lighting. If you have none, you should keep your opinions to yourself and let somebody else place the lights. Lighting should complement the mood of the movie— working with the story, not against it. A mystery should have lots of shadows and contrasty lighting. Conversely, a screwball comedy should be very brightly lit, and not too contrasty.

We all know that the director of photography is in charge of lighting the scene, but you as the director are in charge of telling him how you want the scene to look. On a lot of sets, the chemistry between the director and the director of photography will set the tone for the film. I cannot stress enough how important it is to have a good working relationship with your director of photography. Keep in mind that you can't start filming until all the equipment is in the proper place, and the person who is responsible for getting it there is the director of photography. If your DP is a slow lighter and you are a fast shooter, you might find yourself getting very frustrated. Some directors want the flexibility of having their actors free to roam the set, so they can be spontaneous. If your DP lights in a style where it is crucial for your actors to hit their marks, well, let's just say you might not be able to see your actors very well. The important thing to keep in mind is that all these approaches are valid; it is just a matter of finding a DP who works in a style that meshes with your own.

Cheap Lighting

Natural light is both beautiful and cheap. You will get the best lighting in the morning and late afternoon; this is because the sun is low, which makes for nice shadows that will result in a contrasty image. In addition, sunlight in the morning and in the late afternoon casts a warmer hue—again, a desirable effect. In general, it is best to place the sun behind your character's back or to one side; this will result in a nice rim light, giving the image an edge. From there, the next step is usually to bounce some light back toward the actor from the front, with either a white card or a gold or silver reflector.

During the middle of the day, when the sun is directly overhead, the lighting will be flat. Another undesirable result of the light coming from overhead is deep shadows around your actor's eyes. To combat this, use something called a twelve-by-twelve frame with a butterfly. The **twelve-by-twelve frame** is just that: a metal square that measures twelve feet on each side. The butterfly sits inside this frame. It is made of translucent material and will diffuse the light coming through it. You want to fly this butterfly overhead so the sunlight passes through it, thus softening the light being cast down on your characters. Then you can place a light somewhere behind to cast a nice edge light; again, you can either bounce some light back in from the front or set up a light for this purpose. The final option would be to go inside and shoot some interiors during the middle of the day.

Murder Mystery

To achieve contrasted lighting, use harsh, directional lighting. Light everybody from the side and don't use any fill light. It's that easy—or is it? Harsh, directional lighting results in a harsh, unbecoming light illuminating your characters. While this might be fine for the evil villain whose face has been pockmarked by years of childhood acne and then several cycles of Accutane, it might not be something your leading ladies will appreciate. There are several devices available to soften directional lighting; most of these are composed of a boxlike structure placed over the front of the light with several layers of diffusion within the box structure. This is also known as an **eye light** and produces a nice glowing light concentrated around your leading lady's eyes.

Comedy

The key to lighting a comedy is to give the actors a little more room than usual to operate within. You see, most comic actors will come up with some of their best bits or line deliveries on the spot as the camera is running. So if you have only given them a limited range, and they move out of it to deliver the comedic performance of a lifetime, you're not going to get a second chance. One way to achieve this is to take all your lighting units and point them toward the ceiling. The resulting bounce light will fill the room with a soft, even light. There is no need to limit yourself to bouncing lights off the ceiling; you can also set up white cards or use part of a wall. The basic idea is to bounce the light, thereby softening it and dispersing it over a wider area. This gives your actors additional leeway in hitting their marks on the set.

Girls

Unless you have cast some supermodel, you should avoid direct light on the females in your film. Chances are you have given your girlfriend the lead female role, and rightly so. (While she might be the apple of your eye, others might find her mole-covered face and harelip a little disturbing.) So be kind in your lighting. Generally, you should light women from eye level slightly off to one side— the subject's *better* side. Cover the light with lots of diffusion materials. If that doesn't smooth out your subject's skin, you might want to put a fog or ProMist filter over the lens. Or just shoot her from far away, or only in crowd scenes. If this doesn't work, give some thought to recasting the part.

Guys

Men can take harsh lighting. It will enhance the rugged, manly features your hero possesses. Hit men with direct, undiffused lighting off to one side.

Bad Guys

Light these unscrupulous meanies from below. It will heighten their demonic look.

TECH NOTE: **When shooting film, remember that over-exposure is good, underexposure is bad. Try to overexpose by one stop.**

TECH NOTE FOR VIDEO: **Underexposure is better. Once you overexpose video, you cannot get the information in the overexposed area back. You can, however, pump up the video level and reclaim information lost in the shadows.**

American Cinematographer Manual

This small red book, not to be confused with Mao Tse-tung's little red book, is often referred to as "the Bible" by some rather pretentious cinematographers. This book is full of charts and tables and the various wavelengths of different lighting fixtures. The beginning of the book has a little section on all the different motion-picture cameras available. If you look up the camera you have rented, the manual will tell you how loud your camera is in decibels (dBs), but it will say nothing about how to use the camera, much less load its magazines. This book also contains some outdated articles written by members of the American Society of Cinematographers (ASC) on such things as Arctic filmmaking and filming underwater—both things you will likely encounter. The most useful thing in this book is the depth of field charts located in the center. Using these charts, you will be able to determine what areas of your scene will fall in focus and what areas will be out of focus for the focal length of the lens you are using.

HINT: **The American Society of Cinematographers has changed the cover of its book to green. Although Mao might not approve of this color change, the content is essentially the same.**

The Art of Choosing Film Stock

For economic reasons, you will be shooting your film on 16 mm. Some of you will say, "We should be using 35 millimeter." Others will say, "I can get just as good an image with Super 8." Those of you who think you can shoot it on videotape, meaning VHS or 8 mm, Hi-8, or even DV, please return this book to the store for a full refund. Just kidding. Feel free to skip this section, though. Sure, 35 mm has four times the picture area of 16 mm, but in order to get that you must pay four times the price. Since the primary market for your film will be either the film festival circuit or the home video market, it just doesn't make sense to spend the extra cash. Both of those outlets embrace 16-mm films.

What about Super 8? Sure, the Kodachrome film stock looks great, but let's get real here—its EI is 40. What are you going to do, shoot the whole film outdoors at noon? No way! The film will still look worse than it would on 16 mm, and you don't ever stand a chance of blowing up your film to 35 mm. That kills one of your dreams—movie fantasy number five, seeing your film projected on the big screen—so let's forget about Super 8.

Several crucial factors will go into choosing the proper 16-mm film stock. Will you be shooting interiors or exteriors? By day or by night? Most important, how much cash do you have on hand? Say you are going to make your film on a 3:1 shooting ratio. This means that for every minute of film that makes it into your movie, you will shoot three minutes of footage. Throw away 2 and keep 1. Some quick math will tell us that a 400-foot can of film runs for 11 minutes, but let's call it 10 because of the waste at the front and at the end of each roll. Therefore, to make an 80-minute film, you will need 8 cans multiplied by 3, our shooting ratio, for a total of 24 400-foot cans.

Go to your ATM and request an account balance from your savings account. Take this number and divide it by two. Next, divide the remaining number by a hundred. The number you are left with is equal to the number of cans of 16-mm film you can afford. If this number is under twenty-four, you should check if a credit line is available to you.

Savings account balance ÷ 2 = _____ ÷ 100 = _____ cans of 16-mm film

The cheapest way to get film stock, short of absconding with an Eastman Kodak truck, is to buy it used.

Used film comes in three varieties. One type is called **unopened** because the cans have never actually been opened. Another type is called **recan** because the can has been opened and then the film was put back into it, or recanned. This is a logical name for an item associated with film production—a rarity. The third type is called **ends**, which is the section of film left over after a roll is partially used.

Ends are the cheapest type to buy, but they have certain drawbacks. Because they are short lengths of film, you will have to change magazines more frequently. Also, the film has been handled at least twice. It was first loaded into the magazines and partially shot. Then it was taken out of the magazines. But if these two facts don't bother you, then by all means use ends; just try and steer clear of lengths under two hundred feet.

The second most economical film stock is recan. These are full four-hundred-foot loads that come from music video and commercial shoots. On big commercial jobs, the camera assistant may load up ten mags at the beginning of the day. The mags that are not shot are unloaded at the end of the shoot and put back into their cans—thus the term *recan*. Recan is a good deal. The price falls in between that for ends and unopened film, and you get the convenience of full four-hundred-foot loads. However, large quantities of recan are difficult to find.

The third type of used film is known as unopened stock. It is just that: film stock that was purchased by a production but never opened. This type of film stock is not very cheap; you will pay about 10 percent below what you would pay for factory-fresh stock. Unused also has the same inherent dangers of recan and ends: You don't know how long it cooked in some PAs trunk in some desert while he was probably off playing video games or buying CDs with the production company's petty cash.

When it comes to buying film stock, use your own discretion.

If you are buying your film from a middleman, remember that he might have tested each roll of film by ripping off ten feet from the head and developing it. From there he could take a density reading of the negative and get a pretty good idea of the freshness of the negative. If you see a totally black strip of film taped to a can of recan, avoid it at all costs.

Of course, there is new factory-fresh film stock. You can buy this at about $125 per roll from Kodak or Fuji.

HINT: **Buy American.**

If you're going to buy new stock, I would stick to Kodak's new Vision film stocks: 7279 for low-light situations; 7274 for indoors when you can get big movie lights; and 7245, the fine-grained daylight-balanced stock for day exteriors. These stocks should make shooting a breeze. And you will not be contributing to the trade deficit. On the other hand, Fuji makes a good product; moreover unlike Kodak, Fuji is willing to adjust its pricing. If you can get a deal, you might want to shoot Fuji.

Color Temperature

Color temperature isn't just about a water faucet with a red handle for hot and a blue one for cold. Film stocks are balanced for two color temperatures: **tungsten,** which is 3,200 degrees Kelvin, and **daylight,** which is 5,500 degrees Kelvin. If you shoot a tungsten-balanced film stock outside without a color-correcting filter, your film will take on a bluish look. This is because film stock is sensitive to the blue spectrum of light. Film stocks balanced for daylight have been formulated to compensate for this shift toward the blue and will accurately reproduce color outside.

Conversely, if you shoot daylight-balanced film inside, you will get a shift toward orange; if you look closely at an indoor light or a tungsten light, you will see that they seem to cast a warmish glow. Light streaming in from the window is colder, or blue. This is another way people express the color temperature; they might say they want it warmer, or if they want a stark look they might say colder. Which film stock is right for you?

Choose Tungsten

The easiest film stocks to work with are those balanced for tungsten lights. Then, if you need to shoot outside, you can use a number 85 filter in front of the lens to correct for the film's oversensitivity to blue light. The 85 filter is orange, and it will decrease the amount of light reaching the lens by two-thirds of one f-stop. This is one of the main reasons for using tungsten-balanced film. Say the film stock is rated at 200 ISO. Inside, you will probably be shooting at somewhere around a 2.8 on the lens. When you move outside, you are going to drop in the 85 filter. **Drop in** means placing the filter in front of the lens. It's a technical term that a lot of DPs use. Keep in mind that drop in really means check the filter for any scratches or smudges, then carefully clean it off, and then slide it into position in front of the lens. With the 85 filter in place, your film's effective speed is now 125. If you were still shooting inside, you would be shooting about an f-stop of 2, a speed most lenses can't reach. Even if they could, you would have a very limited depth of field. However, once you move outside, you have access to something called the sun; therefore, you should have plenty of light, and shooting with the 85 filter shouldn't be a problem.

What if you want to shoot daylight-balanced film inside? Well, that is a bad idea. The fastest daylight film has an ISO rating of 250. To shoot this film indoors, you are going to need a special filter called an 80A. This crazy filter will bring the ISO of your film down to 64. That's right, down two stops. Trying to get enough light into an interior location to shoot with such slow film is a nightmare. So repeat after me: "Tungsten-balanced stocks for interiors and low light situations. Daylight-balanced stocks for outdoors."

To summarize:

Tungsten-balanced stocks are used for interiors, low-light sets, or outdoor shots with a number 85 filter.

Daylight-balanced stocks are used outdoors only.

Other Filters You Might Need

Filters are fun, and in some cases you just can't get by without them. There are several filters that you should have with you at all times. The first group is called **neutral density (ND).** These filters produce no change in the color of light reaching the film; instead, they decrease its intensity. If you are shooting a medium-speed film outdoors on a sunny day, the meter might tell you to close your lens down to T-45. The only problem is that your lens only closes down to a 22, and that makes you two stops short. To compensate for this, you can throw an ND 6 in front of the lens. This will decrease the amount of light reaching the lens by two stops and thereby enable you to get the proper exposure. In the ND filter numbering system, you divide by 3 to get the number of stops the filter takes out. For an example, let's take an ND 9. Divide 9 by 3; that equals 3, which is the number of stops that filter will take out.

Suggested Filters

ProMist filters come in either black or white. With the black, you get more contrast; with the white, you get more of a blooming effect when you shoot toward a light source. These filters come in varying degrees, ranging from the lightest, 1/8, to 5. You would probably not use anything over a 1/2.

If you want a really deep-blue sky, a **polarizing filter** is the only way to go for the most effect. You will actually see the sky darken as you move it around. The polarizer can also take glare out of glass, so if you need to see through a car windshield, this is the filter for you.

These are the basic filters you will encounter. Your DP might have his own favorite, but just be sure to have him explain the result they will achieve if you are unsure about what they do.

I'm Hungry

Next to film stock and all the costs associated with it, your second-highest cost will be food. Perhaps the most difficult thing about making your film will be keeping the cast and crew fed. The best possible solution is to bring your mother to the set and have her take care of all your crew's nutritional needs. Unfortunately, in the twenty-first century, most moms have jobs. That means that besides directing your film, you will be in charge of catering.

A couple of days before the shoot, hit the local supermarket— or better yet, one of those discount food clubs. Grab a cart and fill it with tons of pasta, rice, and some beans. For breakfast, pick up a large industrial-size tub of margarine and about a hundred bagels and one rectangle of cream cheese (just a token effort here). OK, go to the meat section and get some processed hamburger patties and some hot dogs. Somewhere in the middle of your shoot, you will spring this all-American meal on your cast and crew, who will react with shock and amazement. In addition, you will need a few pieces of fruit, maybe some oranges, so nobody gets scurvy.

One note: It's great that you are saving so much money by buying your food items at a discount club, but don't be tempted by the absurd. I was on a shoot where the producers were so cheap that they actually bought a bag of bread heels. That's right. No middle section of bread, just the heels. This was a knockout blow to morale on the set, and the crew would not eat these heels or the generic Hostess Ring Dings called Rounds. So throw a little caution to the wind, just don't piss windward. Nothing can destroy crew morale faster than starvation. If you are forced to decide between a rebellious crew or buying a couple of extra hamburger patties, go for the chopped meat.

Lunch is relatively easy. All you need are cold cuts. Ask the guy at the counter to slice them paper-thin. If you can't see through the meat, it's too thick. Bologna is the cheapest acceptable lunchmeat, but you should get a bunch of different types so that people can complain when the one they want runs out. Get the standard condiments, a big bag of chips, and a couple of pieces of fruit. That's lunch.

Dinner should be your big meal, and it will almost always consist of pasta. It is filling and nutritious—perfect for the marathon runners in your group. Most important, it's dirt cheap. Thus, the **Pasta Principle** is a rule you should live by.

What else do you need? Coffee, tons of coffee. Remember that no matter how much food you make, it will never be enough.

There are also a select few foods that should be avoided. For instance, chili and beans and franks are on the list of no-nos. Anything that is likely to produce a rearward expulsion of gases (i.e., a fart) should be avoided. Few things can shut down a movie company faster than a few well-placed barrages of natural gas. Imagine the poor dolly grip who has to push the camera operator who just gorged himself on the frank and beans buffet. Get the drift?

Long after America is gone, far into the future when space kids are studying history, their professors will point to a map of what was the United States of America and ask, "Kids, what was this country's greatest contribution to mankind?" Little Joey will undoubtedly answer, "Ketchup and Doritos." Make sure you have these on your shopping list.

Another crucial skill to develop is the proper navigation of the salad bar. I call this the meat-in-the-soup-container maneuver. We all know that when you heap piles of food into your little plastic container, you are going to pay for every leaf of lettuce because the scale at the cash register doesn't miss anything. But yes, there is an option. Think soup. That's right: When you buy soup at the salad bar, no matter what size, it is not weighed. Now if you pack that soup container full of the beef Stroganoff, you could walk out with three to four pounds of stewed meat for the same price as a pint of split pea soup. Two or three of these containers over a box of Minute Rice and you have fed your crew of ten for about ten bucks. I would say that's a good deal. Remember to rest your hand on the soup container while you check out so that any overzealous clerks can't feel the weight of the container; and while you're at it, ask for a spoon and skip the bag, because you are going to eat this in the car.

Vegetarians

Any crew member who requires a special diet should be avoided. Don't get me wrong. I wish I could eat properly, but the special requirements of vegetarians cost both time and money. Hummus and couscous are expensive and hard to find. When you are on location, you want to run to the corner deli, order a bunch of cold cuts, and be done with it. I, for one, don't want to run around looking for organically grown tomatoes while I could be filming a key scene for my movie.

Recipes

Here are a few tried-and-true recipes guaranteed to save you a buck and satisfy a hungry crew. Remember that cooking is also an art form; don't be afraid to express yourself in the kitchen.

JOHN'S BEEFY MACARONI

John says this one is great for the film crew on the move. He starts with two pounds of elbow noodles. No need to bring the water to a boil, just toss them in the pot. Once the noodles are the right consistency, he adds cheese (any old cheese will do).

Next, cook up one hamburger in a frying pan. John says this is more of a psychological meal then anything else. The greasier the meat, the better. Chop the patty into micropieces and sift them into the macaroni pot.

Your cast and crew will think that the other guy got all the meat. In order to perpetuate this hoax, you should, at every given opportunity, hail the chef and remark that your portion had more meat in it than macaroni.

2 pounds of elbow noodles
1 package of any old cheese
1 hamburger patty

STEVE'S COLD PASTA SALAD

Steve first cooked up this culinary delight on the set of the film *Deadline*. He starts with two pounds of swirly pasta, which he cooks up. He then throws this into a large bowl, to which he adds several cans of chickpeas or pinto beans, whichever happens to be on special that week. To this he adds tuna fish. He salts and peppers the dish liberally, then covers it and throws it in the fridge. Steve recommends serving the dish cold with a Rolling Rock beer to wash it down.

2 pounds of funny-looking noodles
2 cans of beans (which were on **sale!***)*
2 cans of tuna fish
1 Rolling Rock beer (optional, this is for the cook)

CHICKEN SOUP SANDWICHES

Take a whole chicken and throw it into a pot of boiling water. Add all the old vegetables and any other leftovers you have lying around. Let this cook for a long time. When the substance in the pot resembles a thick paste, it is ready to eat. Get a slice of white bread and butter it liberally. Scoop some of the soup solution onto the bread; fold over and it's ready to eat.

1 chicken
Lots of leftovers
1 loaf of Wonder Bread

Remember: Eat these babies fast, before the soup can eat through the bread.

CHEF TELL'S PASTA WITH ONE MEATBALL

This little recipe was whipped up by the TV chef himself for yours truly while we were shooting *Road to Park City*. It's a fast, simple way to feed a crew of twenty. Dump the pasta into a large pot and bring it to a boil. Be sure to overcook the pasta; that way it will absorb more water and get bigger. Drain the water and pour in the red sauce. Then top it with one meatball.

20 pounds of pasta
1 quart of red sauce
3 ounces of meat

LITTLE DEBBIE'S STAR CRUNCH CAKES (OR, THE ART OF KRAFT SERVICE)

Most people despise this dessert, so if you can develop a taste for these mutant rice crispy treats, you will be in the catbird seat.

How many times have you walked past a major film shoot that has taken over an entire neighborhood for its own purposes? As you walk past the grip trucks and Winnebagos and all of the other assembled equipment, you might have seen a couple of folding tables set up. These tables are covered with all kinds of munchies— everything from cookies to bananas, with a few novelty items such as chewing gum and gummy bears thrown in. Past this pot smoker's munchie-attack paradise are the tables themselves. Yes, it seems they are covered with a nice seamless sheet of thick brown paper. This paper is called **kraft paper.** So what do you suppose these tables of food are called?

Yes, you have arrived at the **kraft service table.**

OK. One, you are coming back. Two, you can't remember what the tables are called. Three, you will not remember the paragraph above. *Snap.*

Get some bags of cookies and maybe some chips and throw them into the kitchen somewhere. If people have time to snack on your set, you are not working them hard enough.

HINT: **People love to complain. By supplying them with the lamest foods known to man, you are providing them with great conversation pieces.**

Coffee

Filmmakers, like policemen, require large amounts of highly caffeinated coffee. However, the brewing instructions on your can may not be up to the standards needed to get a film crew through several twenty-hour days. A general rule is to double the recommended amount of grounds for each pot you brew. If the spoon does not stand on its own in your cup, the coffee is probably too weak.

In this day and age, some people are going to be looking for a double skinny mocha with two blues. You don't have the time or the money to indulge your cast and crew with a double anything, so be careful not to set a dangerous precedent. Offer coffee and, if you feel nice, milk and sugar.

Doughnuts

Unlike policemen, filmmakers do not require this greasy dough covered with sugar and decorative sprinkles. Instead, filmmakers prefer bagels. Doughnuts are a sure sign of a student film. Perhaps younger filmmakers have not developed the stomach problems that plague a large portion of the filmmaking community. In the real world, film professionals eat bagels, especially bagels with cream cheese. The good thing about bagels is that yesterday's throwaways become today's breakfast after a quick trip to the microwave.

Finally, that leaves crullers. A cruller is a doughnut, but it's straight. For some reason, in every group of ten, one guy has to ask for a cruller. Now this is something you can't take lying down. Today a cruller, tomorrow the world. If anybody asks for a cruller, ask how a cruller is any better than a doughnut. Then walk away.

Nō-Dōz

These little caffeine pills should be used only as a last resort. They tend to upset the stomach and make one edgy. If you can get your caffeine fix from coffee, you will be much better off. And yes, to answer your question, you can snort Nō-Dōz. They have a pleasant minty taste, which is followed by a mild burning sensation.

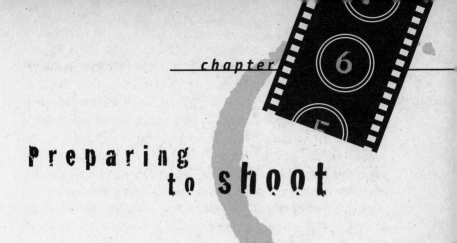

Preparing to shoot

> *T*he more time you invest before the shoot, the easier
> the actual production of your film will be. So get off
> the couch and get to work. **—*FRED OTT***

Script Breakdown

Before you shoot your script, you must break it down into more
manageable units. Go through your script and give each master
scene a number. A master scene has an INT. or EXT. header, followed by a brief description of the scenes and/or locations, as well
as the time of day the scene takes place. Sequentially number each
master scene in the left- and right-hand margins. Don't worry if
two scenes take place at the same location—they should still each
get their own number. Wow, that was easy!

Now it's time to make a breakdown sheet. Grab a blank piece

of paper and draw six columns on it with the following headings: Scene #, Location, Cast, Pages, Props, and Special. Under Scene #, write the scene number (as it corresponds to the number you wrote in the margin on your script). Under Location, write the location where the scene takes place. Under Cast, list the characters that appear in that particular scene. Under Pages, note how many script pages this particular scene will run, rounding to the nearest eighth of a page. (This helps later in determining how much time will be required to shoot this scene.) Under Props, list any props needed in the scene. Under Special, list any special requirements the scene has, such as day for night, a special effect, or anything else you can't forget to bring to the set that day.

From these breakdown sheets, you will prepare the shooting script. The shooting script differs from the script in that it's in the actual order that you will shoot the scenes. It details which scenes are shot on which day and estimates the amount of time required to complete each scene.

First, group together scenes by their locations. Start with scene one. Let's say its location is a beach. Go through your breakdown sheets and list *all* scenes that take place on a beach. Go through the entire script and group scenes together in this manner. You have just broken down your script by location.

Next, count up how many pages of script must be shot at each location. In order to complete your film in ten days, you need to shoot at least nine pages of script a day.

Now decide in what order you will shoot these scenes. Scenes taking place at sunset and outside should be scheduled either very early or very late in the day. On the other hand, a sunset scene that takes place indoors can be shot at any time. You should shoot the major scenes before the smaller ones. Use your own judgment. Every film has its own peculiar needs, and every location has its own set of rules that you may have to bend in order to get the proper shots.

The final step is assigning a specific shooting day to each location. This is usually dictated by location availability or actor availability. When completed, this second breakdown will be a blueprint for shooting your script.

Coverage

In Hollywood, the cost of film stock does not make up a substantial portion of the budget. This means that Hollywood productions can afford to do hundreds of takes from many different angles in order to cover a scene.

For you, film stock can easily represent a third of the budget, so you must tread lightly. There are a thousand ways to shoot a scene, and everyone may have his or her own ideas about the proper approach. But remember that you're constricted to a shooting ratio of 3:1. If you do three takes of the any one scene, you've used up all the film allocated for that scene. Try to limit yourself to one take from each camera setup. If something goes wrong, then do a second take—but make sure you get it right.

Your first shot of any scene should be a master shot that takes in the whole scene and all the dialogue, with the camera on the person or people speaking. This still leaves you with enough film to do two more passes on this particular scene. You could move in and do a close-up of each actor (assuming there are two), covering each for the entire scene.

Or you could decide that you'll let the master shot run for half of the scene and that you won't need a close-up until the end of the scene. So you cover the second half of the scene in matching close-ups. This leaves you enough film for one more complete pass.

Or you may want to add flair to this all-important scene. Maybe dolly in on a key piece of dialogue. Or get a close-up of the ring, a symbol of your hero's affection and commitment. Leave yourself room to get creative. It will really help your film's production value. The most important thing is to make sure you have enough coverage before you get to the editing room.

If something goes wrong with the camera or a light explodes in the middle of the take, it's OK to shoot another (thereby going over your shooting ratio for the scene). Just make sure this doesn't become a habit. Another film-saving technique is to shoot a scene in one long take. If you rehearse the scene you might get it on the first try, and then you can use your second take as a safety and then save the film from the unneeded third take for another scene.

Safety Takes

What is a safety take? After you shoot a take that you like, some-one may request another one, and you'll have to determine if it is needed. The safety is in doing another take just in case. The soundman may be unsure if he actually heard that jackhammer dur-ing the last take, so he'll ask for another take for safety. Or the director of photography may have missed his cue and not panned to the butterfly as it landed on the protagonist's nose. These are the times when you will hear the words "Let's do one for safety."

Before you give the go-ahead to this potentially time- and film-wasting action, first question the crew member. Find out why he or she feels the need for the extra take. If the crew member confesses to a blunder, then do the safety, because in this circum-stance it's not really a safety—the first take's unusable. However, if the crew member requests another take "just in case something happens to the film at the lab," then not so fast. Sure, once in a while the lab accidentally destroys a roll of film. But if they do, then guess what? Yup, that's right. Your so-called safety will be just as ruined as the first take. The safety take is sometimes valid, but keep in mind that if a take is perfect except for one small sec-tion, you could always do a close-up or wide shot that would enable you to edit around the mistake and solve the problem with-out wasting film stock.

The Pie

To determine how long it will take your crew to set up a particular shot, think of your film set as an apple pie. If you only want a small slice, it should be relatively quick to set up the camera and lights to film in that section. However, as you get hungrier for a larger slice of pie, you will need to allocate more time for the crew to set up. The bigger the slice of pie the actors have to work in, the smaller the slice you have for hiding lights, dollies, and microphones. And as the pie slice increases, it complicates things because you will have to put up more lights. More lights create more unwanted shadows, more light spills, and more heat. Start out with small slices of pie and gradually work your way up to the huge dinner-size slices that look so good in the display cases at your local diner but always disappoint the palate.

Turn It Around

It's often surprising to beginning filmmakers how much time it takes to light a scene. Keep this in mind once an area of the set has been lit. The best utilization of time would be to shoot everything that takes place in this area, regardless of when it occurs in the scene or script. For example: You're shooting a king sitting on his throne. In the first shot, the king says, "Off with their heads!" In the second shot, the prisoner stands before the king, reacting to his sentence. In the third shot, you dolly in on the king as he says, "Now."

First you should light the king and his throne. Then shoot the first and third shots. (You should also keep in mind any other throne scenes that appear in your script. If the king reads from an ancient scroll in a scene that appears at the end of the film, shoot it now.) Then relight the room in the opposite direction for the second (prisoner) shot. Minimize the number of times you take down and move the lights. The more you move the lights, the less time you have to shoot.

The Cheat

You are going to hear this word a lot, especially from your director of photography. Say you have two characters holding a conversation in a living room. Character A sits on a couch that is against the wall and which faces Character B, who sits in a chair in the middle of the room. The first shot looks at Character A, on the couch, from over the shoulder of Character B. After you cover all of Character A's dialogue, you want to get a matching shot of Character B (from over the shoulder of Character A). Now you realize that the only way to get a matching shot would be to knock out the wall behind the couch so you could get behind Character A and shoot over his or her shoulder. Or you could "cheat the couch forward." Since film is two-dimensional, nobody in the audience can really tell how far the chair is from the couch or from the back wall. So move the couch away from the wall and get the camera behind it to shoot Character B.

There are many types of cheats. Other popular ones concern characters' eye lines. Even though your character is talking to an actor directly in front of him, this does not mean that he must truly look at that character. The basic concept of any cheat is this: If you haven't shown the audience the exact geometry or layout of the room or location, you can move objects in or out in order to make the shot more pleasing to the eye.

Matching Shots

Let's go back to the conversation between Character A and Character B. When shooting an over-the-shoulder or head-and-shoulders shot of one character, you will want a matching shot of the other.

The key word here is *matching*. This means that Character A's head and body must fill the same proportion of the shot/screen as Character B. This is known as **matching your shot,** and it will lend a subtle, professional feel to your film.

Walk in, Walk Out

If I learned only one thing from an egotistical director of photography who was teaching a bunch of retards about filmmaking in a Connecticut city known for being the birthplace of the three-ring circus, it was the importance of starting every shot with the character walking into frame and ending every shot with the character exiting—known as the **walk in** and the **walk out.**

It doesn't matter if the character ducks out of frame by reaching down to tie his shoe or if he exits through a door. Whatever you do, get him out of there. Keep this rule close to your heart and you will thank me a thousand times as you edit your footage. The idea is simple: Give yourself an editing point (i.e., a logical place to make an edit) at the head and tail of every shot. It's a safety valve. If all other editing attempts fail, you can always go to the walk out.

Production Value

Production value is money spent on the film that can be easily noticed "up on the screen" by your average theatergoer. In Hollywood, it might be by trashing a Ferrari Modene 360 (with the F1 shifting option), or by filming a cast of thousands who are waving hockey sticks and charging into battle across sand dunes in a post-nuclear civilization.

For you it's the difference between renting the Yugo or the Nissan. Or it could be something as simple as fresh flowers on a table. Production value is important and should never be overlooked.

Exploit and capitalize on any opportunity to trick people into thinking that you mortgaged your parents' house to shoot your film. Here are things you can do to make your film look more expensive: Buy your friend's junker car and light it on fire. Sprinkle interesting dolly shots throughout your film. Don't limit your film to all exteriors or, conversely, all interiors. Get permission to shoot your scene at the local historic mansion or rent that Cessna for fifty bucks an hour and shoot a couple of aerial shots. Even if you only use these **money shots** for the opening or closing credits, it will still make your film look like it cost more than $10,000 to make.

How to Trick People into Doing Work

It's the end of a busy, hectic day, and you don't feel like building a mount that will enable you to hang the camera from a bungee cord in the center of the room. Now is the time to get your crew excited about doing work they are totally unqualified to do. You should have a rough idea of the strengths and weaknesses of your crew; the PA who always seems to trip on the fifty-foot extension cord would probably not be a good candidate to build something you will rest a $20,000 camera on. The PA who got you into your car after you locked the keys in it might just be your man.

Once you select your prime candidate, here's a proven technique that will result in the desired response: Pull over one of your crew members and ask (as if he were the only person in the universe with the answer), "How would you make this rig?" As he explains how he would do it, feign interest. Get very enthusiastic. Finally, "remember" that you have to be doing something else right now (this isn't a lie; you'll *always* have to be doing something else). At this point your "expert" should volunteer to build the rig for you. Walk away quickly before he has a chance to reconsider. Other phrases you might consider are "What would you do?" and "Would you hold this for a second?" *Never* underestimate the importance of "Would you hold this for a second?"

Seduction on the Set

Let's face it. A major reason you got into the film game is for sex. OK, this isn't entirely true. You have a unique vision you want to share with the world, or you have the need to express yourself through a visual medium. But the film set is a lonely place. You have primal needs, and they're usually magnified when you spend a great deal of intimate time with a small group of equally lonely film people.

So how do you seduce the starlet, or that brainless beefcake who spends a little too much time admiring his own ass? After a long day of shooting, nothing tastes better than a beer. So here's your first move: lots and lots of alcohol. Like at frat parties, there's nothing like liquoring somebody up in order to have your way with them. Another thing to keep in mind is that a film set is an opportunity to reinvent yourself. Just like when you entered college, no one has preconceived notions of you on a film set, and everyone will quickly stereotype you the minute they lay eyes on you. So ask yourself, "Who do I want to be on this set? Am I going to be aloof and untouchable, or down to earth? Am I going to be the strong, silent type who knows everything but refuses to say it?" Once again, remember the importance of beer. Any beer makers out there want to sponsor this book? Imagine your brand name preceding the title!

The Zoom Lens

The zoom lens is an extremely dangerous thing in the hands of an amateur. Usually as soon as Joe Filmmaker discovers the zoom, he is immediately "zooming in." Or "zooming out." Then he attempts the "zoom in" and "zoom out" in the same shot. Or some "crash zooms." Or the Hitchcockian "dolly out zoom in." Or, conversely, the "dolly in zoom out." Until every shot in the film has a zoom effect. This is annoying, so keep it in check. Like anything, if you have a certain effect you wish to accomplish and a zoom gives you the right feeling, then zoom. Just make sure you use zoom shots at an appropriate time and place in your story.

A Word About Special Effects

Special effects cost big bucks. This cannot be avoided. Minimize scenes with the gigantic alien mother ship or the exploding anything. A good car explosion, however, might be worth it. All it takes is one and it will look great in your film.

Space Ship on a Stick

If you must do that space opera . . . remember rule one of Space Ship on a Stick: Don't show the stick. Keep it dark—the less they see, the better off you will be. Rule two: Shoot in slow motion. That will smooth out any jerky movements you may make as you pull the fishing line attached to the five-inch-long battle cruiser you constructed from model airplane parts and balsa wood.

Fake Blood

You may need it, so make your own. The secret? Karo syrup. This stuff can be found somewhere between white sugar and baking soda at any supermarket. The other ingredient is red food coloring. Mix the syrup and the food coloring together and you instantly have real-looking blood that's safe to drink. Go ahead, take a sip.

Don't Believe Everything You Read

What about all those nifty ideas shared by professionals in the latest issue of *American Cinematographer*? Buyer beware! Some time ago there was an article that described a "poor man's Steadicam": Take the camera (which you rented and is worth $20,000). Mount it in the center of an eight-foot-long two-by-four. Then, with a man holding either end, run down the street with your subject.

How do you frame a shot? No one's looking through the camera or riding on the two-by-four. And I don't know of any eight-foot-wide unobstructed sidewalks, do you? Imagine running down a crowded street holding this rig. No working cinematographer is going to give away his secrets. He'll just get a big laugh when he sees the report on the evening news that "twenty people were killed when a one-hundred-pound ARRI BL mounted on a ten-foot stick went berserk in midtown Manhattan."

Gathering

> Preproduction is like a scavenger hunt, a very expensive one. **—JOHN ICANT PAYRENT**

That is exactly what preproduction is: a scavenger hunt. Make a list of everything you need for your film. Then find each item for the absolutely lowest possible price. Congratulations! You're not just running errands anymore; you are filmmaking! Buying stuff takes on an entirely new meaning. Gone are the humdrum days of going to the store to pick up some lunchmeats—now you're going to the supermarket to make your movie!

Props

Read through your script. Every time you come across a prop or a set piece, circle it in red. When you're finished, make a list of all the circled props. You should have them assembled before filming begins.

Let's talk about firearms, because they are very common in scripts—and very dangerous. Do not count on finding an Uzi submachine gun at the last minute at your local A-Z rental store. There are a variety of prop houses that will rent you a very convincing replica of a firearm. If the gun doesn't need to actually fire, this is preferable. If you absolutely need to see a muzzle flash or an ejecting cartridge, get a gun that fires blanks only. Keep the gun locked away, and only bring it to the set when needed. Even though it may fire blanks, treat it as a real firearm. The rules: Do not point the weapon directly at anyone. Check and double-check to make sure it's empty between uses. Finally, keep it locked up.

Wardrobe

When you cast your film, tell your actors that they will be responsible for supplying their own wardrobe. Tell them how you see their characters and make some clothing suggestions. If they need a special piece of clothing, make sure they don't spend too much to get it. No $55 Armani tank tops. The best place to find wardrobe is a thrift shop or Goodwill. The price is right, and the racks are full of all kinds of unique finds. If your script takes place in the 1960s or '70s, all the better.

Plan on seeing your actors' wardrobe choices before the first day of filming. You don't want to waste valuable time later locating the perfect fish tie.

The Tech Scout

Before your first day of shooting, schedule a crew meeting. Invite the department heads to your house and tell them it should only last an hour. Once everyone arrives, quickly herd them into a large vehicle and drive them to every major location. This is the tech scout.

A representative from each department (camera, sound, art, wardrobe, etc.) should be in attendance. At each location, discuss how you envision the scene or shot. Your crew will then explain what they need to make your vision a reality. In the process you may discover that some locations won't work. A room may be too small, or the available light may not hit the window correctly. The tech scout gives you a chance to get the proper equipment you need to proceed smoothly.

Finally, during the tech scout, if anyone suggests getting lunch, tell him or her you have a dentist appointment and drop him or her off immediately. I cannot stress this point enough, so I ask you to repeat after me: "I will not go to lunch with my crew." Why? If you go to lunch with your crew, you will have to pay for it. When the check is on the table, your crew will suddenly turn into mentally challenged quadriplegics. They will sit with their hands at their sides, staring at you stupidly and smiling. Not a pretty picture. You will have no choice but to pick up the tab. So go ahead and schedule your tech scout, but first schedule that dental work you've been putting off for so long.

Gaffer's Tape

You can't have enough of this stuff. When problems arise on the set, chances are it can be fixed with gaffer's tape. The bigger the problem, the more tape you'll need to fix it. Props can be made from this tape. I have seen ties and knives made from it. It comes in every color. Use a roll with some colored Sharpies to make quick and easy signs and labels. Use black gaffer's tape on **hot** (filmed) **sets**—it will be harder to identify on camera than gray gaffer's tape.

A word about the shiny gray duct tape: shiny gray duct tape will *not* work on set. Yes, it's cheaper, and the yellow duck on the package is cute, but the adhesive on duct tape is a mess. It will not be kind to walls or furniture or anything it sticks to. Gaffer's tape will. Pay the extra cash and get the real stuff.

Better yet, work a couple of days on somebody else's film set and hoard rolls of gaffer's tape for your own movie. On big-budget movie or commercial sets, a roll is not considered good for anything once it's been half used, so drop these **short ends** into your duffel bag. Then hand them out to the gaffers and grips on your set and watch morale soar.

When Crew and Actors Bail

The phone rings. It's the actor who's playing David, the lead in your movie. His voice wavers as he explains that he's leaving in an hour on the late train to Kalamazoo, Michigan, to perform with a dinner theater troupe for the next six months. Needless to say, he will not be available for your movie. You need a new David.

What do you do? Remain calm. Look through your headshots and your audition tapes and make a list of possible replacements. Hang Old David's headshot on your dartboard. When you have your list of New Davids, swallow your pride and call the first one on your list. Although I rarely recommend honesty, in this case it's the best thing to do. Explain to your potential New David that "some SOB, a moronic, subtalented, pencil-necked actor-geek who will never amount to anything or work in this town again" backed out at the last minute. Ask the New David if he could take the next week off from his day job to play the bumbling detective lead in your movie. If he can't or won't, call the next victim and repeat the spiel until somebody says yes. Then go celebrate with a game of darts.

Film Jokes

Be the life of the party with these mildly amusing exclusionary jokes that only "film people" will understand:

Q How can you tell when a Teamster is dead?
A *When the doughnut falls out of his hand.*

Q How can you tell a Teamster's kid at recess?
A *He's the one watching everyone else playing.*

WARNING: **Teamster jokes (in the presence of Teamsters) may be hazardous to your health.**

Q How many PAs does it take to change a lightbulb?
A *Who cares, but while you're up there could you paint the ceiling?*

If you want more of these jokes, then buy my next book, *Film Jokes for Film People*. If you have any jokes and would like to see them in print and would like to receive absolutely no money for them, then e-mail them to me at howtoshoot@hotmail.com.

The shoot

How to Spell Relief

It's the night before your first shooting day and you have a million things to do: prepare your shot list, inventory your equipment, recharge the camera batteries . . . it's mayhem. And then your best friend from high school calls. He wants to go out and slug down a few beers. There is nothing you'd rather do than get away from the three-headed beast that is otherwise known as **Your Film,** but you must exercise discipline. _Don't do it!_ Don't go out partying during the shoot. There will be plenty of time to drink beer and sing the blues during the editing process. I recommend jogging during preproduction and production. Jogging increases stamina, which is what you need for those sixteen-hour shooting days. Once principal photography is completed, then you'll have time to develop your drinking problem, call your shrink, or hit the streets in pursuit of illicit substances. But for now you're going to keep healthy, so hang up on your high school buddy and get back to work.

The night before day one, get as much done as possible, but realize that you will never get everything done. So set a cutoff time and make yourself get at least two or three hours of sleep. You are going to wake up with a stomachache after your first of many consecutive sleepless nights. Do yourself a favor and have Rolaids near your bed and a couple of rolls in your pockets. Filmmaking spells stomach disorder, guaranteed. The industrial-sized jugs are the best buy and come in many flavors.

Personal
Hygiene

Don't hit the snooze button! When you roll out of bed, make sure you shower, shave, and brush your teeth. Take care of yourself now, because this will be your last chance to take a personal inventory for quite some time. Filmmaking takes its toll, and usually the first thing to go is shaving. Once that's gone, showering is not far behind—so have deodorant handy. A vital location for any director is the bathroom. This little cubicle will become your sanctuary. It's a place to review the script in complete privacy or to formulate strategies on how to deal with crew members. This is not a time or place to peruse the latest *People* magazine or *National Enquirer*. If you must read, stock a good supply of technical books. When you need to solve a problem, retreat to your "office" and do the necessary research. Finally, the tank above the toilet makes a great cooler and hiding place for your beverage of choice, so fill it with the knowledge that no one will pilfer your supply of JOLT cola on this shoot.

Baseball Caps

You need at least three of these caps to shoot a feature film. When the oil in your hair reaches thirtyweight, it's time to switch caps. One of the caps should be film related. It could be a Panavision or a Mole Richardson hat. It should display the registered trademark of a film-related company. Your second hat should display the logo of your favorite professional sports team. If you don't have a favorite team, select one from the list below:

Oakland Raiders. You are a tough, free-speaking filmmaker who is not afraid to express his opinions.

New York Mets. You are from New York and proud of it, but you're still showing your independence by not jumping on the George Steinbrenner bandwagon.

Los Angeles Lakers. This is more of an actor's cap, but it means you want to be Hollywood ASAP.

Miami Dolphins. Who can resist the cute little dolphin on this team's insignia? (They also happen to be the author's favorite football team.)

Buffalo Sabres. You are an individual and angry about it. You know you will fail, but you will be buoyed by your hatred of the system and mankind.

You have a little more leeway with your third cap. It can display a joke, though these are more becoming on grips and electricians. Or maybe you want it to bear the name of the film you are making. Go to your local mall and find that stand-alone booth, the one in the middle of the walkway where you have never seen any customers. It's between the cart that prints up fake newspapers and the one that pierces your ears for free if you buy a pair of exotic $2.99 earrings. Wake up the high school girl who works there and request that *Freaks from Hell* be stitched on a black cap. The hat will be ready in minutes. The golden rule: *Never* be caught wearing the same cap two days in a row.

Growing a Beard

If you've never grown a beard and you're the director, you might want to try. Beards are often associated with intellect. Think Steven Spielberg, Francis Ford Coppola, or Martin Scorsese in the 1970s. Once it fills in, people may treat you differently. Unfortunately for female directors, people *will* treat you differently.

On the Set

OK, you've arrived at the location on day one. The Rolaids are working their way through the small intestine, battling stomach acid at every turn of this snakelike organ. Time to make a film. The first thing you do is drink a cup of coffee, even if you don't want one. This is a time-honored tradition that goes back to the days of silent movies. While drinking it, engage in useless chitchat with those around you. Talk about your mutual fund. Ask about a new piece of equipment you read about in some trade journal. Then excuse yourself so you can get down to business.

Go to your first location and decide how to shoot your first scene. Involve your crew in this process. They may have many helpful suggestions and some really bad ones. It's up to you to sort it out. Decide where the camera goes and tell the assistant camera-person to get it there. Then talk to your director of photography about lighting the scene. He will give you an estimate in hours of how long it will take to light it. Take this time estimate, cut it in half, and tell him that's how long he has to work with. It's up to the DP to marshal his team and work on the technical aspect of filmmaking while you slip away to deal with the actors. Actors will bring an onslaught of questions for which you better have the answers. The actors will come up to you with ideas about how they want to play the scenes. Consider what they say and then, based on your vision, decide if it's appropriate behavior for their character. If it seems in character, encourage them to explore it. If it feels wrong to you, pull them back and suggest another approach more to your liking.

On the first day, you have to deal with all the little details that slipped through the cracks during preproduction. While it may be a little overwhelming, remember that it's only going to get easier. The first day is also essential because it sets the tone for the rest of the shoot. In order to make sure the first day goes off without a hitch, schedule a scene you are sure you can complete. Falling behind schedule on the first day sets a bad precedent. Also make sure that you don't physically wear out the cast and crew on the first day. Make yourself finish work on day one in ten to twelve hours. Slaving fourteen or sixteen hours on the very first day will wear your crew out. Save the longer and harder days for the end. You may have to work twenty-four hours straight, but you can push on, knowing that the shoot is nearly over and that you can sleep the following week.

Blocking

Keep the crew busy. In order for your comrades to do their jobs efficiently, they must know what's going to happen in each scene you are shooting and where it's going to happen on each particular set. This is known as the **blocking.** Blocking is the choreography of people and camera; it's when and how they move. The actors, of course, will want to know *why* they move; they will want motivation. You can go from a simple wide-angle static shot to an ultracomplicated dollying crane shot with your actors doing pirouettes and backflips as they move from point A to point B. The more complicated the shot, the longer it takes to set up. Remember that time is money. So strike a balance. If you keep your camera and actors stagnant and shoot everything in wide shots, besides showing no flair and announcing to the world that you are unimaginative, your production value will decrease. So be creative. Work closely with your DP when blocking. If you have access to your locations before you film, try to spend some time there with your DP. Together you can walk through the scene and devise a plan. Once the DP gains an understanding of what you want, he can go about the business of setting up the shot while you work with the actors. It is crucial for all crew members to understand what is going on. Everybody from the prop people to the caterer (yes, even your mom) can benefit from knowing.

Action

You're ready. The scene is lit, the actors know what to do, and your stomach has finally settled. Here it goes. First, yell "ROLL SOUND!" Always roll sound first; it is cheaper than film. When the sound is up and rolling at proper speed, the soundman will yell "SPEED!" That is the cue for the assistant cameraman to read off all the pertinent information on the slate—namely, the scene number and take number. Then yell "ROLL CAMERA!" The camera operator will turn on the camera and yell "SPEED" when the camera is running up to speed. That is the cue for the AC to slap the slate closed and quickly scurry back behind the camera. Now (drum roll please) yell "ACTION!" The actors will begin. You're making a movie. After the scene is over, yell "CUT!" The camera and sound will stop, and that's it. Go again, or move on to the next shot.

The Line

This is the most misunderstood and most mysterious beast in film-making, but it must be mastered if you wish to become a competent filmmaker. When you shoot your master shot, you establish a certain geography for your audience. For example, the Amazon Lady is on the right of the screen looking left toward the man in the monkey suit. Now, if you cut to a close-up of the Amazon Lady and she is suddenly looking right, you have crossed the line, and your audience loses its sense of screen direction. There is an easy way to avoid this mistake. Place all your actors at their proper marks on set. With chalk, draw a line connecting the two actors who are closest to the camera. Extend this line to the walls of the room. (Be sure you can't see the chalk line in the frame.) While you shoot the scene, keep the camera on one side of this line and *do not cross it*. Thus, your screen direction will stay consistent and correct. If you cross this line, then you become an avant-garde filmmaker. Avant-garde filmmakers watch Andy Warhol movies, wear black, and pray for subtitles. They order venti-skim-chai-iceddecaf cappuccinos with whipped cream at movie concession stands and are totally put out when they can't get one. Don't let this happen to you. Don't cross the line.

Cutaways

In addition to covering the actors as they speak their lines, there are other shots you should get for each scene that aren't part of the main action. These are known as **cutaways** (as in "cutting away" from the main action). Cutaways are your friends. They make life much easier in the editing room.

Examples of cutaways: the hands on a grandfather clock showing the time; the television or a computer screen; that beautiful vase that you broke by accident while moving the camera between takes. If possible, shoot different objects on each set for each scene. If you didn't get coverage of a character crossing a room, simply cut away from the character to a shot of something in the room, and then cut back to your character, who has now magically shifted across the room. Cutaways work best when they show something pertinent to the story or if they contribute to the visual style of the film. Either way, getting plenty of them in production will save you time and money in postproduction.

The Slate

The slate is a highly popular and visible symbol of the filmmaking process. And you've waited a long time to get your hands on this piece of equipment. What does it do? The slate allows the editor to synchronize the sound track with the picture in each take. That way the actors say their lines in sync with their mouths when they move on screen. Slates mark the beginning of each filmed take. They display the scene number, take number, the director's name, the DP's name, the camera op's name, and (oh, yeah) the name of the film. Often the name of the movie will change during the shoot. And less-than-flattering nicknames for the director may appear on the slate as well. Don't worry, this is natural. Slates also tend to disappear for days on end. You will know this because the camera assistant will be clapping his hands in front of the camera like a slate in order to mark the scene. This is known as **guerrilla filmmaking.** As long as the arms are in frame, this method works.

Camera Placement

Where do you put the camera? Always shoot the speaking actor's face. Always. You may not show that actor speaking in your finished film, but you need to get photographic evidence of it now. Even if the camera is upside down and mounted on a crane and dollying over the edge of a cliff, as long as the lens is pointed toward the person speaking lines you have the correct camera position. If two people speak in a scene that involves complex person-and-camera choreography, work hard to catch each character saying his or her lines.

Low and Wide

The set looks awful, or else you're using yesterday's kitchen as today's study because a location fell through. Your camera operator can't leave the bathroom because he's been drinking coffee all morning. He had the camera doing quadruple axels and triple flips the day before, and now you've fallen behind schedule. You need hard and fast work today. What will you do? Easy: Take the camera and put it on the floor, widen out the lens as far as it will go, and shoot the scene looking up at the actors. Not only will your actors be in focus, but you will also avoid having to see the horrible set. In addition, you have introduced a stylish angle into your film. It's a win/win/win situation.

Director's Equipment

While searching for the perfect camera shot, never form a rectangular film frame with your fingers. You'll just look obnoxious. And

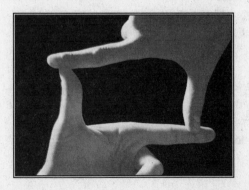

unless you have Spielberg's budget, don't go and place a special order for a camera viewfinder with a gold chain and zoom for half your movie's budget, either. If you want a director's viewfinder that badly, go to a CVS and buy some disposable cameras. They may be made of cardboard, but you'll get the same results. Now you can take pictures with your "viewfinder" and also have still photos from the production of your film, thus saving money by not hiring a stills guy.

Continuity

When you cut from a wide shot to a close-up, it's reasonable to expect that the furniture in the room will not change position. This is known as **continuity.** If stuff starts to move around from shot to shot, you have no continuity. This usually happens when actors hold things in their hands—like a drink, for instance. Since actors are not machines, they never do things exactly the same. They may drink a little faster in a wide shot than in the close-up. When you cut from the close-up to the wide shot, the glass may appear to have more liquid, or less. Or the water may have turned to wine. Or the glass may have become a hamburger. Is this a problem? No, and here's a reason why: people love pointing out these faults in films. It makes them feel superior. Entire books have been written about how the third storm trooper hits his head on the door when R2D2 and C3PO are discovered in the Death Star in *Star Wars,* or the "dead" flying monkey that's tangled in a tree in a wide shot in *The Wizard of Oz.*

So provide your audience with mistakes. Then, after the movie, when the house lights have come up and the celluloid dream dissipates, and the people in the audience return to their dreadfully boring and grossly insignificant lives, they can rehash all the continuity errors in your film with each other and feel better. The more continuity errors, the more lost souls you're saving. Feels pretty good, doesn't it?

Check the Gate

After saying "CUT" at the end of a scene, and before moving to the next camera setup, you should turn to the AC and say, "Check the gate." He will then pop the lens off the camera and look into the camera's gate (where the film is housed). He is looking for hairs, emulsion buildup, or any other crap that may have worked its way in between the film emulsion and the lens, thereby creating an unwanted image on your film. If there is a foreign element found, you need to clean it out of the gate and, if possible, reshoot any affected scenes. But be objective when deciding whether or not to reshoot a scene. Time, money, and resources are in the balance. Sometimes it may be impossible and you are stuck with what you have. In these cases, mutter under your breath, "We'll fix it in post." That means you hope it fixes itself by the time you get to the editing room.

Room Tone

Two seconds after you yell "WRAP" at the end of each shooting day, the soundman will respond, "Wait, I need room tone. Quiet please." By now you've learned that the soundman is not to be trifled with. He's more finicky than a vegan housecat and twitchier than a Trekkie losing his virginity on his fortieth birthday, but in his attempt to make your film audible, he's not fooling around. Room tone is important. It may be the most important thing in all of filmmaking. Bigger than you, and certainly bigger than your stupid little movie. Thus, for thirty seconds you and the entire cast and crew *will* stand perfectly still in utter silence while the soundman records the sound of "one hand clapping"—that is, the location you are standing in and its absolute essence. You do not want to stand between a soundman and his room tone. Trust me, you'll find out.

Talking with the Actors

While the crew is busy setting up and lighting the next camera shot, talk to the actors. Go over the scene you are about to shoot. Discuss wardrobe with them and talk hair or makeup. After this small talk, proceed to talk about the characters, their motivations, and all the other little details that will enable them to embody their characters truthfully. Your discussions with the actors should be an open give-and-take. Tell them your ideas about their characters and then give them a chance to express their own opinions. Refer specifically to what's in the script. Accept one or two of their ideas that make absolutely no difference in the outcome of your film. This makes the actors feel better. Reject a couple of ideas outright to remind them who is in charge. Smile a lot; talk with your hands and nod at everything. Don't listen to what they are saying. Because what they are saying has something to do with why their character should open the door with their left hand and not their right.

When you've devoted as much time as you can stand (or two minutes, whichever comes first), check your watch and say, "That jerk should have had this set lit an hour ago." Then run off. You have not only put on an admirable acting performance yourself, but you have officially qualified as an actor's director. Never blame an actor for anything, even if it is her or his fault.

The Secret to Directing Actors

There is no secret, no magic bullet when it comes to directing actors. Everybody takes a different approach. All that matters is achieving the desired result on film. To do that you must understand how each actor works. And each actor works completely differently, with completely different languages and methods. Try to understand where actors are coming from. Understand what it's like for them on set—not simply their on-camera work, but the sitting around and waiting, or the repetition of the work. Be sensitive to their psyches or egos. At various times during the shoot they'll need a friend, boss, parent, bartender, or psychiatrist.

What other advice is there? Mostly technical. If you're making a low-budget film, make sure the actors understand your 3:1 shooting ratio. The actors must strive be on right away, with no room for improvisation or error. Try to schedule rehearsal time with your actors to train them for the tightrope walking of the actual shoot. Don't direct them—with line readings, for example—except to give them technical advice, such as moving them in or out of frame.

Here's a low-budget technique that helps later in the editing room: during a two-person dialogue scene, ask the character who isn't speaking to turn his head, look away, and then look back at the other person. This will give you more options when editing. You can cut to a character's **look back,** which adds importance to what is being said by the speaking actor.

The Release

Before filming takes place, have every one of your actors sign a release form. And *every* means any person that is photographed or put on film—including your mother and the owner of the toy poodle you borrowed. This piece of paper should grant you, the filmmaker, the right to use the actor's pictures, voice, likeness, and anything else connected with them as it pertains to your film for as long as the film exists (forever). Each of you should then sign and date the form.

If you don't have a release form on location, have your soundman record your conversation with the actor. Getting it in writing is more reliable from a legal standpoint, so insist on eventually drawing up the paperwork with every actor.

Sex Scenes

Shooting love scenes can be awkward. I used to try and save these scenes until the middle portion of the shoot. I surmised that the actors would be more comfortable with each other and the crew by that time and thus be more at ease. I have since learned that the best time to schedule love scenes is on the first day. On the first day the actors are more eager to do good work. Everyone on set believes he or she is making *Citizen Kane* on their first day. That your movie will win every major award. That the actors will rocket into the $20 million salary club and onto the A list. Your crew will talk about working on your movie as if they had a religious experience. Reality hasn't set in on the first day, so you can get your crew and your talent to jump over the moon for you.

However, if you wait until the second week of filming to schedule your sex scene, the actors and crew have sized up the project. After a couple of days, the crew and actors have already ascertained whether a film is noble or of high quality and have predicted its chances for success. When you ask for that topless scene now . . . You will get the response, "Can I leave my bra on?" The only problem is that this question is not really a question at all. It is a condition, and like it or not, you are going to be short one T-and-A scene in your film.

And if you thought sex was tricky in real life—it's dark, you can't get the bra strap off, you're thinking about baseball—wait until you encounter the technical problems with filming sex scenes. The actors are scantily clad or naked, making them uncomfortable. The actors are joined by at least a dozen staring crew members, making *them* uncomfortable. The actors will be lit brighter than an exploding supernova, making them more uncomfortable. And you will be shouting instructions to your actors while they pretend to have sex, making them more uncomfortable yet. You'll wish you were back in the dark.

Improvise Only If the Camera Is Not On

You have a very limited amount of film stock. There's no time for experimentation while the meter's running. During rehearsal, it's OK to explore alternative readings and blocking, but at some point you must decide what feels right for a particular scene and shoot it in that manner.

You will *not* be able to shoot it both ways—that is, the way you want it and the way your actor wants to try it. It will only complicate things and may potentially render other scenes already completed incongruent. Settle on one version of each scene and then shoot the scene that way. It is your job as the director to settle on the best way to shoot a scene, so figure it out and stick to your guns. Don't hedge your bets by shooting alternative versions.

Wear 'Em Down

You have a very specific idea about how you want a crucial line of dialogue spoken. Unfortunately, your actor also has his own ideas. After a discussion with your actor, you feel your solution is better, but the actor insists on doing it his way. Let him. After each reading he gives, shake your head and say, "That's not working, try it some other way." Offer him no solutions. Do a few more rehearsals, rejecting each attempt as ineffective. When your actor throws up his hands in disgust and says, "Well, how would you do it?" show him the way you wanted it done in the first place.

Film Slang

Much like the Royal Order of the Water Buffalo and the Friars, film-makers have their own secret language. This language was invented to totally confuse novices trying to break into the industry. Large men with insatiable bagel habits derive great pleasure from using these nonwords in front of newcomers to show how much they know about clothespins, metal screens, and rope.

FILMMAKER-TO-ENGLISH Dictionary

Steel Pieces of wire mesh you place in front of a light to lower its intensity; also known as *scrims*.

Number 2 Wood Clamp (or C-47) A clothespin. Really.

Hi-hat A seat for the tripod head that stands about five inches high and is used for extremely low shots. This is a good example of a word meant to confuse the film novice. *Hi-hat* would definitely send the novice searching for the highest set of legs for the tripod.

Stingers Extension cords.

PC Petty cash.

Doodads Can be anything. Really.

Black wrap Outrageously priced black tin foil.

Inky A small two-hundred-watt light.

Cuckoloris A piece of cardboard riddled with holes. It is placed in front of a light to simulate trees or venetian blinds or whatever you cut the pattern to be.

Cheater That little plug that gets rid of the ground; also known as a *three to two*.

Forgery

If you are pressed for time and cannot get the proper signatures or permits, you might want to sign the papers yourself. The trick to forging a signature is to do it in reverse or upside down. I think you will be very pleased with your results.

They Shoot Spies, Don't They?

If you are conducting a guerrilla shoot, first equip yourself with the proper attire. Drive down to the closest college or university. Find the campus store. Pick up a few T-shirts that prominently display the school's name. You might also want to get a baseball cap to add to your growing collection. When you're shooting, make sure somebody is wearing one of those college shirts. The authorities will assume you are some stupid students who don't know any better and might not hassle you. You may get off with only a lecture, or by writing a scene for a cop who's always secretly wanted to be an actor.

Stupid Stuff You Need to Know

Blip Frames

These are the overexposed frames at the beginning and end of each shot as the camera winds up to speed or down to a stop. But don't let it stop there. Whenever you see something humorous on the set, you should immediately train the camera in that direction and squeeze off a couple of frames. Believe me, these will make your stay in the editing room more enjoyable.

Obligatory Movie Quote

Once you begin shooting, start uttering a quote from a movie. Repeat this quote at least five times a day. For example, you might choose "Not unless round is funny." Repeat it over and over. Give it some time. People may act annoyed or puzzled, but you're the director so they have to listen. Before long, the set will be abuzz with your quote. You are a god.

Righty Tighty, Lefty Loosey

This rule applies to not only Home Depot (great people, those Home Depot folk) but to all film equipment. Yes, even the stuff manufactured in France. Turn knobs, screws, fasteners, and bottle tops to the right and they get tighter. Turn them to the left and they get looser or pop off in your hand.

Ferraris

People love to see these red sports cars in movies. Find a way to sneak one into your film. You might try your local country club or that auto detailing shop around the corner. Why not ask one of your production assistants to get a job as a valet parking cars at the country club? He may get fired and consequently do serious jail time for grand theft, but not before supplying you with a steady flow of exotic vehicles that you can film for a couple of hours at a time. If you put actors in the car, you have gone a long way toward making your film a commercial success.

Cops

If (your budget is less than fifty grand) and *when* the cops come calling, treat them with respect. Cops like a good ass-kissing as much as anyone. Explain that you're shooting a movie. When they ask for your permit say, "Did I need one?" Tell them you are a student. Identify the PA wearing the NYU sweatshirt as the person in charge.

There are several other good strategies when it comes to dealing with members of law enforcement. Check around in your cast and crew and see if anybody in your group has a relative who is a policeman and have them do the talking. If the cops are friendly (or even if they aren't), ask them to drive through your shot with their lights on.

Jail

The whole point of this book is to keep you out of jail, so pay attention. Let's say the cops really, really didn't like you. Call your parents. Cry. Claim a medical disability. If nothing works, try a bail bondsman. And don't forget to use this as a publicity stunt. If you do go to jail, get plenty of pictures and definitely notify your local newspaper about the recent arrest of a local filmmaker. Those pictures and news clippings will be invaluable later, so make sure you hang on to them.

Weird Is As Weird Does

Being weird for its own sake is not going to help your movie gain critical or commercial acclaim. Weird is the world of bad rock videos, *Twilight Zone* episodes, and avant-garde experimental films. Weird is good for short films running ten minutes or less. People tire of Day-Glo sets, strobing light effects, goofy super-wide-angle shots, and unmotivated camera movements.

Stills

These are ultraimportant when it's time to put together some kind of publicity package for your finished film, so make sure someone is constantly taking pictures on set and during the filming of actual scenes, because you cannot afford to be without these. You should assign somebody the specific responsibility of shooting still pictures on the set. Load them up with a mixture of black-and-white and color film and check out the first couple of rolls to make sure they are up to the task. The first thing you need to make is a poster with some great stills. The first thing your distributor will ask for is twenty good stills. You need stills for the video's box cover. Film festivals always request stills. When the press calls to do a piece, they'll ask for stills. Your mother wants a recent picture of you; surprise her with some stills. Get the picture? Good—then make sure you get the pictures.

Where Did That Light Meter Go?

This is absolutely guaranteed to happen at least once during your shoot. Everything will be ready, but the DP was busy preparing lunch, and now he cannot remember where he put his light meter. Well, if you're inside, just open the lens up as far as it will go (2.3 if you're lucky, 2.5 if your lens is a little older, 2.0 if you went for the German zoom). If you're uncertain about going on without a light meter, think back over the last few days of the shoot. What f-stop were you shooting at? That's right, 2.8, wide open, or maybe at f4 when a lot of daylight was flooding through the windows.

If you are outside, then it's time to use the F-16 rule, and I don't mean the jet fighter. On an average sunny day, if you are shooting film with an ASA of 50 at 1/50 of a second, then your exposure will be F-16. Don't believe me? Then grab that light meter and head outside. While you're out you might want to get some of those cheese-covered nachos at the local minimart.

"Wrap"

You will find yourself alone. Immediately after uttering this word. That's because when you wrap, you're done filming, but your work is just beginning. **Wrap** means putting everything back exactly how you found it and where you found it, just like in kindergarten. Crew members have booked flights to Antarctica in order to avoid the wrap. So what must be done? First and foremost, return your location to its preshoot condition. To do this, there are a myriad of miracle solvents, glues, lotions, and creams that can be bought at your local fix-it emporium. Put your trust in these products; they are your friends. Cameras and equipment go back to the rental houses. Rental vans and cube trucks go back where they came from. All the furniture is put back to normal. A useful trick learned in college: Use white toothpaste to cover up the holes in the walls.

chapter 8

Digital Video

Welcome to the video revolution. You are going to shoot your feature film on video and in the process save yourself thousands of dollars. The drawbacks? Well, there are a few, depending on whom you talk to and on what day. The obvious drawback of video is how your image will look. Video images have a different quality than those shot in film. Film tends to be warmer and more organic, while video seems to be sharp and bright. These observations were the results of countless focus groups conducted by myself in preparation to write this paragraph. They are countless because they equal zero.

While your average viewers will not be able to tell if you shot on film or video, they will sense a difference and may psychologically assign some lower value to your project. But most television viewers would be hard pressed to tell the difference between film and video. On the other hand, there is a group who can tell the difference, they are known as film snobs. Film snobs will instantly belittle your project the minute they find out you are shooting it on a video format, no matter what. Just write this off and keep on plugging ahead.

The other thing to keep in mind is that video is an entirely different animal than film. It has both its drawbacks and its pluses, but before you can exploit any of these attributes it's important for you to know how exactly video works.

How Your TV Works

Right now your TV plays back its picture at 30 frames per second (fps). Thirty separate pictures shown in quick succession give you the illusion of smooth motion when you view a television. Each frame contains two fields of video: the upper and the lower. You are never actually seeing a complete frame of video. First you see the upper field, which shows you only the odd scan lines on your television; then you see the lower field, which shows you the even scan lines. This process is called **interlaced** because you are only seeing half the picture at a time, either the odd or the even scan lines on the television, and then you see the first field of the next frame as the cycle repeats over and over again. So your television is actually playing at 30 frames per second, or 60 fields per second. Got it? Good. Because here is another little point. Although everybody says your TV is running at 30 fps it is actually running at 29.97 fps.

29.97 and What It Means to You

A long time ago black-and-white televisions ran at 30 frames per second, and then one day along came a thing called color television. People who had just bought a top-of-the-line seven-inch black-and-white television were not about to throw away their sets (much to the chagrin of the television industry), so the broadcasters had to develop a way for these older black-and-white sets to be able to receive and broadcast the newer color signal. In 1953, the National Television Standards Committee (NTSC) came up with a plan. They figured that by actually broadcasting at 29.97 frames per second instead of 30 frames per second they could use the extra .03 of a second to send some additional information to make their color signal work with all televisions. Thus was born the great timecode dilemma that we all enjoy so much today.

Timecode Drop and Nondrop

It should be no surprise to any American that we insist on using 29.97 frames per second as our standard video playback rate. Just as we rejected the metric system, we also reject a simplistic frame broadcast rate.

Now that we know that our television is running at some weird frame rate, it brings up another interesting dilemma. In order to edit and keep track of a show's running time, there is something known as timecode. **Timecode** expresses the position on a videotape as hours, minutes, seconds, and frames. Let's say the first frame of your show is assigned the time code of 00:00:00:00, the very next frame would then be expressed as 00:00:00:01. If you are an hour into the show, the timecode would read 01:00:00:00. Now we have a problem, don't we. Remember that the frame column is advancing 1 digit per frame until it reaches 29, then it cycles back to 0 and the second column advances to 01. But our show is not actually running at 30 fps. It's running at 29.97, so when the timecode reads 00:00:01:00 (or 1 second) we have actually only viewed 29.97 frames per second: We are .03 frames short. Somebody has cheated us out of that .03 frame. Over time, this could add up to a lot of minutes. So our friends at the Society of

Motion Picture and Television Engineers (SMPTE) came up with something known as **Drop-frame timecode** as the solution to our vexing little problem. Drop-frame timecode works by dropping the :00 and :01 at every new minute mark except at the 10-minute mark and every interval of 10 minutes. This amounts to 108 frames dropped per hour, or 3.6 seconds of screen time. Thereby, drop-frame timecode can keep track of a program's actual running time.

Now that we know what timecode is, you should always record tapes with **non-drop-frame timecode**. When you master your program to tape, you might consider using drop frame but again I would lean toward the nondrop. Unless you are delivering a master to some television station that demands drop frame so it can get an accurate running time of your film, I would steer clear of drop frame.

PAL

Now that you know all about American televisions and frame rates, let's take a look at the utterly absurd European standard known as **PAL**. In Europe, all televisions run at exactly 25 frames per second. In Europe, all film cameras run at exactly 25 frames per second. In Europe, timecode runs at exactly 25 frames per second. So I ask you, who would want to get involved in this crazy, mixed-up system? I'm not sure why we in America have such screwed-up televisions but I'm willing to bet it has something to do with a lobbyist group and some backroom dealings. Because PAL is running at 25 frames per second, some filmmakers might think it would be a good format to shoot on if one was eventually going to transfer the video to film. Well, you would be right about that. However, I would caution you against this because of the difficulties of finding PAL editing equipment and the lack of experienced facilities to do the actual transfer to film. In short, it's a great idea but difficult to implement.

Video Formats

If one more person says "I'm shooting a film on digital video" to me, I think I'm going to blow my brains out. No, there is nothing wrong with it; let's just call it what it is. Digital video (DV) is a consumer product with a picture resolution roughly equivalent to Betacam SP, the stuff they shoot your favorite TV tabloid or news show with. It is by no means some miracle product like the FLOBE or DD7. You will see that if and when you are lucky enough to blow your video up to film. Now that I have gotten that off my chest, let's talk about the various video formats and all they have to offer us.

Right now there are no fewer than ten digital video formats in distribution, with new ones coming out faster then you can say built-in obsolescence. So let's go down the list and examine what camera makes sense for your project.

Before there was digital video we were all told that HI-8 and super VHS were going to change the video world as we know it. Well we now know this didn't happen and because of this very fact I would avoid these two formats. Let's just call them formats of last resort.

DV

First, let's examine all the DV formats. This includes DV, DVCAM, Mini DVCAM, DVC PRO, and probably a few other DV formats that are only available in Japan. All these formats are essentially the same. They are what most people are shooting when they say, "I'm shooting digital." The picture quality is actually quite good on these cameras, and the sound can be, too, if you take the time to get it right. Also, these cameras have modern features that can be of some assistance in the editing process. The tapes are cheap, and some of the better units have interchangeable lenses. One of the most popular cameras is the Canon XL-1. It would be a good choice because of its many features and the ease with which you can manually override many of the automatic features.

High Definition

On the other end of the spectrum is high definition (HD), also a digital format. The new cameras from Sony can shoot at either 30i, the video standard, or at 24p. The p stands for **progressive scan,** and to explain this we are going to need to back up for a second. We all know that video has two fields per frame, with each field showing the viewer half of the television's scan lines at a time. The 24p is a video format that mimics the way film records an image. The P stands for progressive and what this means is the video is not interlaced. This means the viewer will see both fields at once. The 24 means that the video is actually running at 24 fps, just like a 16- or 35-mm camera. So what is this good for? You can't watch your video on a standard TV this way, and even if you could the picture tends to flicker because of the slower frame rate and the noninterlaced video. However, if you were to transfer these videos to film, you would begin to see the advantage. One frame of full-screen video would equal one frame of film. For this purpose and this purpose only, shooting in 24p would be advantageous. But— and this is a big but—if your video is not going to be transferred to film, you might be making big headaches for yourself during the editing and final postproduction stages. Also, if your video doesn't get transferred to film, you are screwed.

Betacam

Then, there are the old standbys Betacam SP and Digital Betacam. Both of these formats are field proven. They have been around for many years and have become the standard in broadcast production for at least the last ten years. The cameras are reliable, and the equipment is available at most rental houses. If you go this route, you should rent a Sony 600 to shoot Betacam SP; for Digital Betacam it's the 700 you will be renting.

Let's look at what all this means to you and me, because I am also easily susceptible to the hype surrounding the latest and greatest video gear. Just like all other equipment freaks, I could find myself going down a path from which there is no easy return. So don't be so quick to grab the newest video format—there could be ramifications you are not ready to handle.

The formats I would consider shooting are as follows (in descending order):

Hi def (either 30i or 24p)
Digital Betacam
Betacam SP
DV Pro
Mini DV
Digital 8, Super VHS, or Hi 8

To decide what video format is best suited for you takes a round of phone calls. Call everybody you know and find out what kind of video cameras they own and if they will be needing them in the month of June.

Chances are slim that your uncle has a Betacam in his beloved camera bag, but he might just have a mini DV camera, and if he does, that is going to be our move. In fact, for the purposes of this chapter let's assume that mini DV is the format you will be shooting on.

Sears

Did you know that Sears has a liberal return policy? You bet; it's thirty days. Now, remember that you can shoot a feature film in ten days. Do I really need to say anything else? Yes, I do. Keep the packaging and don't fill out the warranty cards; also, leave all the stickers in place on the camera and cover over them with gaffer's tape. You should also cover the edges or any place on the camera that is likely to get wear with a nice strip of gaffer's tape.

When you are done, peel off the tape and gently place the camera back in its box. Here are a few lines to rehearse on the drive back to the store.

"I got two for my birthday."
"The box was already opened when I got it."
"This thing has not worked right from day one."
"Hey, asshole, it's your freaking return policy, so take this camera back and hand over the cash!"

Also, make sure you charge the purchase.

The Camera Is
Small but What You
See Is What You Get

Just because the camera is small does not mean that you shouldn't treat it like a professional piece of equipment. Just because you are shooting on video doesn't mean you can be careless. You have to take the same care with each shot that you would if you were shooting on film. Because you are shooting on video, you have a big advantage in that you can see what the camera is actually recording in real time. You can output the camera to a monitor, so as the DP goes about his lighting, you can actually see what the scene will look like.

The monitor can be both a godsend and a time leech. The other advantage of video is that you can play back a scene after you have recorded it. The problems with this are threefold. First, you have to rewind the tape and then play it back. Then you might rewind it again for a second viewing—but wait, the DP is yelling, "The sun is going down quick, everybody get ready." The DP grabs the camera, shoots the perfect sunset, and guess what? Yup. He just recorded over the best take of the previous scene—the one you exploded the car for, the one you will never be able to duplicate. Yup, that one. Problem number two has to do with timecode. Once the tape is rewound, there is going to be a jump in the timecode after you are done playing back the desired scene. You are not going to want to risk recording over any of your previous shot, especially after you just went through the sunset disaster described above. So after you have viewed the scene you wanted to review, you are going to let the tape play for a few seconds until you reach fresh, unused tape. Now there is a small blank section of tape in between the previously scene you just looked at and the new scene you just recorded. During that blank spot there is no timecode. This becomes an issue when you have to feed the tape into a nonlinear edit system. The third and biggest problem is time. The time it takes to view, review, rewind, reset, and then resume shooting is enormous. Every time you review a take you break the momentum you have gathered up to that point. If you reviewed every take, you would easily cut your shooting day in half. When you only have a little over a week to complete a film, this is a luxury you cannot afford. Now, if you have a technical question or if the take was perfect, but you're not sure if a crucial line was left out by one of your actors, by all means take a look at the tape. Just make sure this doesn't become a habit.

You Touch That Zoom Lens and I Will Kill You

For some reason, the smaller a camera gets, the more people will want to zoom. Zooming is bad, and on a small camcorder it is usually not very smooth. You should make it perfectly clear to your DP that if he wants to zoom, he is going to need to get permission from you in writing, in advance. This policy is absolutely essential when you are shooting on video. I can't explain it, but for some reason somewhere in your dailies you are going to come across a zoom that ruins a perfect take. This policy is an effort to minimize these instances.

Tape Is Cheap

You can keep on muttering that phrase until the cows come home, and in the end it will not help you one bit. Yes, tape is cheap, but time is not. Video has allowed us to overcome one of the most expensive aspects of filmmaking. We no longer have to buy, process, and transfer our film to video in order to see a picture. But we are still saddled with all the other rules of filmmaking—and the primary rule of filmmaking is that it's freaking expensive. So while tape is cheap, filmmaking is expensive. And after you spend a whole day with an actor who demands another take because he feels he could say "Give me the recipe" much better and you oblige because you say it's only costing tape and tape is cheap, you will realize that you just wasted a day of your life and that the only way you're going to get that day back is to pay for it. That means getting the crew back and the equipment and the house and renting the cop uniform and the smoke machine again, plus spending another night baking those little cupcakes with the blue frosting that were so important to the scene.

Video Traps

The traps of shooting on video are many and very easy to fall into. Let's pretend that your video feature project idea is a marshmallow. Now, in the bag of marshmallows there might be a hundred or so of these spongelike sugar puffs. Imagine that each one of those marshmallows represents a neighbor who also has an idea for a video feature film. Now let's go to the campfire. This is where we will turn our marshmallow into a film. Everybody can put a marshmallow on a stick and thrust it into a campfire and burn it to a crisp. And there is the problem. You see, the majority of people shooting videos are going to do just that. They're going to jump into the fire and come out with an oozing, gooey mess they will attempt to pass off as a feature film. Only a few people will take the time and care to gently brown their marshmallows, and these people will have a good film— or at least one that showed a little competence. But you and I know what really happens every time somebody pulls out a bag of marshmallows. Somebody utters the words "If only we had some chocolate and graham crackers we could make a s'more."

What the hell is a s'more and has anybody living actually seen one? I would venture a guess: no. So when you set out to make your film, remember that if you can bring those few extra ingredients to the film set, you, too, can make your video feature a s'more. And because nobody has actually ever seen a s'more, they won't know if you've made it good or bad; but once they taste it they will know it's great, and that's exactly what we are striving for here. After viewing our film we want people to utter "That was great."

Pacing

When shooting video, people start shooting too early, figuring that they can just do take after take until they get the performances they want. But in reality, they may never get the performances they want; they just might get a really well-rehearsed version of the first performance because they never took the care and time to explain to the actors and the crew what they really want out of the scene. This presents another problem, because doing take after take of the master scene often fools people into believing they have more coverage of a scene than they really do. A better approach might be to alter camera angles while one searches for the perfect performance. By using this approach, one can at least cut around the performance and thereby salvage a scene.

Lighting for Video

You should plan on using the same equipment and techniques you would use if you were shooting on film. Just because you can turn on the camera and see everything doesn't mean you are lit. Yes, you have to light the scene to convey the mood of your story. The big advantage of video is that what you see is what you get. You can hook up a color field monitor to your camera and see exactly what each lighting unit does as you place it into your set. One aspect of lighting that is often overlooked is the ability to subtract light. Just as you identify areas of your set you want to see, you should also identify areas that should be dark. You should go about subtracting light in those areas.

Sound for Video

Sometime it feels kind of strange that the mixer feeding the audio to a DV cam is actually bigger then the camera itself, but this just goes to illustrate how important sound is. On smaller video cameras, the built-in microphone should be avoided like the plague. All cameras have an input for overriding the camera microphone and attaching an external source. The smaller cameras have a stereo miniplug; the higher-end gear usually has XLR inputs. If you have a camera with XLR inputs, you are all set. Your soundman will feed the camera just as he would a DAT recorder. If you have a mini, you should rent a little box that has two XLR inputs and a mini output. These boxes will attach to the bottom of your camera using the tripod screw. They allow you to use professional sound equipment with your not-so-professional camera by providing the proper inputs. These boxes also convert the audio signal to the proper impedance so the camera can get a good clean signal. It can then autogain up and down to your dismay. In other words, even if you get the right microphone and the right cables, there is no way to override the automatic sound-level controls built into some cameras. So you will be at the mercy of some engineer in Japan when it comes to your audio levels.

Manual, Manual, Manual

The three most important buttons you can locate on your camera are the manual overrides for the focus, the exposure control, and the audio level.

Yes, you are going to have to focus the camera yourself, but think of the alternative. Say an actor has to pass by the camera, but you want the scene to focus on the character in the background. Well, the good folks at the secret think tank that developed the autofocus program don't know what you are thinking. All they know is that if something big comes into frame, then by God we are going to get that object in focus. And when that object clears the frame, well, we are going to find the next largest object to focus on, regardless of its importance to the scene about Stonehenge and the dysfunctional family.

Manual exposure is just as important for the same reason. You don't want some engineer at Sony telling you how to light your film, but if you choose to leave the camera on automatic, that is exactly what you are doing.

That leaves audio. The autogain is trying to get a nice loud signal that it can record on tape. Again, it doesn't care if that noise is a cricket or a locomotive. Huge shifts in the audio level are most apparent in the background noise level. But all of this should be of no concern because we are going to set the camera's audio level manually, right?

White Balance

Just like film, video is also sensitive to the blue spectrum of light that the sun's rays produce as they are refracted through the earth's atmosphere. To overcome this, video cameras have something called **white balance.** What you do is hold up a white card in front of the lens and then push down on the button labeled white balance on your camera.

The video camera will then take a color temperature reading on the light reflected off the white card. It will then adjust the camera's color balance to that color temperature so that the white card will be a true white.

White balance can be used in a variety of ways to get a desired look. You can trick cameras into white balances that can give some interesting looks. One way is to hold up a colored gel in front of the lens while white balancing. If you hold up a blue gel, the camera will shift its color spectrum in the opposite direction toward amber; the result will be a warmer setup in the camera. Likewise, a coldish tint can be obtained by holding up an orange gel while setting the camera's white balance. Care should be taken when doing this; it is absolutely essential to check the camera's white balance in a monitor before filming commences.

The Bathroom

It's day one. You pull the video camera out of its box, place it on the tripod, and *bingo*! You're not getting any picture. Now is not the time to look like you don't know what you are doing. Grab the camera's instruction manual and retire to the bathroom for what just may become the longest bowel movement of your life. Two things to keep in mind: Don't let anybody see you take the instruction manual with you, and make sure you have a good grasp of how to work the camera before you flush. This technique can be applied to any piece of equipment—or you can use it to get yourself out of unwanted social events.

chapter 9

POSTproduction

*t*he film is shot, and you are exhausted. Before you lie down for a week to catch up on your lost sleep, you have one more chore to do: Get the film into the lab. Grab all the film from the assistant cameraperson. Tape all the cans together into a neat package. Then get all the sound rolls from the sound guy. Grab a cup of coffee, jump into your car (I'm assuming you still have one because you chose this book and not that other one), and drive to the film lab.

Dealing with the Lab

When you drop off your film at the lab, make sure everything is properly labeled. When you fill out a work order, print your instructions clearly. This is not the place to have somebody try to interpret your impressionistic chicken scratch. The lab needs to know what kind of film stock you shot, how to develop it, and what type of dailies you want them to make from your negative film stock. Keep it neat and concise. The lab is going to save every piece of written instructions you give them.

The lab's employees are going to peel the labeling off the cans and save that, too. The purpose? If there is a screwup, they will show you exactly what you wrote when you submitted the film. If the labeling is clear and there is a screwup, they will have to take responsibility. If the directions are murky and open for interpretation, the odds of them taking any responsibility are greatly diminished. It's best to avoid this potential headache.

Dailies

From the original camera negative that you just turned over to the guy with the big thick glasses behind the receiving desk, the lab is going to make something called **dailies.** A production with a good-size budget drops off film at the lab every night. The next morning, the lab returns either the film or the video dailies to the director or producer to screen. You get to see what you shot the very next day. Thus the name dailies.

Today, there are two types of dailies available to the average filmmaker: film dailies and video dailies. Film dailies are positive silent prints made from the original negative film you submitted to the lab. You can look at these dailies on a film projector or flatbed editing table. Video dailies are also made directly from your film's negative, only this time the image is transferred to videotape. As a result, you can look at your film on a VCR and a television. The lab will usually sync up the sound with the picture, so you can also watch these dailies with the location sound. This service will cost money, so pass on this option at this point in your career.

Video or Film? That Is the Question

An important factor in deciding what kind of dailies you want is how you plan to edit them together into your finished film. Your editing process will dictate the type of dailies you have made because you're not going to view film dailies and then decide to edit on video. This would mean making two sets of dailies, and in doing so you would double the cost of this item to you. If you choose video, skip to the next section. If your answer is film, then read this section and be prepared to change your answer.

I'm an Insane Lunatic

Let's talk about some of the good aspects of film. First, its fun to touch and you get to play with tape, markers, those little white gloves that make your hands look like Mickey Mouse's, and lots of other stuff. People like the hands-on feel of film. But you are not making a house out of Popsicle sticks here. You are making a film, and the advantages of video are numerous. When you edit on video, you don't have all these little pieces of film lying around. If you are editing on video, you should then be editing on a nonlinear system such as an Avid or Media 100. These nonlinear editing systems streamline the editing process and will save you countless hours. If you still need the hands-on feel, take a pottery class.

I'm Smart, so I'll Edit on Video

This is the path almost everybody takes today, and with the abundance of computer-based editing systems, I must say it makes a lot of sense.

When you take your film to the lab, you will inform the clerk or technician that you want your film developed only. Since you are editing on video, you have no need for a work print. The lab wants to make money, so it might charge you a little extra to develop only. It might also charge you extra to do something known as prepping for video.

Prepping for video means that the lab is going to splice some leader on either end of your film. The lab might also say that it's going to clean your film, but is it really dirty? Did the lab roll it around on the floor after it came out of the processing machine? Are the technicians using your film as a kitty toy? Is there a dog loose in the lab? Let's get real. Your film should be pristine when it comes out of the developing bath. While you can raise a skeptical eyebrow toward the lab, that is about the extent of your power. Labs are few and far between, and it is in the best interest of every filmmaker to have a good working relationship with one. Moreover, your lab might charge you a little extra if you do your video transfer somewhere else.

All this adds up to a lot of extras, so keep track of these incidental charges the labs are so good at inventing. However, the lab may waive these fees if you decide to let it do the video transfer for you. If this makes economic sense, you may want to go this route. The lab does this to keep as much business in house as possible.

Where Do I Want
to Transfer?

A film lab might cut you a break if you agree to do your film transfer in its own in-house video, or you could take your negative to a posthouse that specializes in video. This decision is going to be totally driven by money. To complicate matters even more, there are different types of video transfers available to you, and each has a different price affixed to it.

The cheapest way to go is the **overall color-corrected transfer.** The telecine (pronounced *tele-sin-nay*) operator is going to take a look at the very first scene that comes up. He will adjust his controls to make this scene look proper. He will try his best to make flesh tones resemble flesh. He will then let the rest of your film run through the machine on this setting. He will do some adjusting on the fly, and if something goes extraordinarily out of whack, he may stop it and correct again—but don't count on it. You can get this type of transfer in the $250 to $300 per hour range. And you will be billed for the running time of your footage, not room time.

Next up is the **unsupervised scene-to-scene color-corrected transfer.** With this one, the telecine operator will adjust the color value of each scene to his preference. You will be billed for room time, usually in the $300 to $650 per hour range. This rate usually depends on the type of machine used to transfer film to videotape and the expertise of the colorist (this is the guy working the machine, and just like baseball players, they vary greatly in skill and speed). When you are paying $500 or so an hour, you can never underestimate the importance of speed. Because the colorist is adjusting the machine for every shot, this type of transfer takes much longer. If you multiply the running time of your footage by three, you will get a rough idea of how long this process will take.

If you opt for either of the these types of transfers, make sure you send in notes along with the film telling the colorist how the film should look, as well as the feel you are going for. If you omit this step, don't be surprised if your night scenes look like day. It is really amazing how easily colorists can screw up the look of your film with a few misconceptions about proper skin tones and by using the dreaded china girl. (A china girl is a pasty white specimen of a girl that a colorist uses as a reference when balancing the colors on your film.)

Finally, there is the **supervised scene-to-scene color-corrected transfer.** Just because you have decided to come to the transfer, they have decided to charge you more money, and it's not because of some unbearable body odor or personality quirk. This is the best type of transfer because you can tell the colorist what each scene should look like as you shuffle through your film. The downside is that this type of transfer builds up a lot of anxiety, especially when you're paying for it out of your pocket. The colorist will get phone calls from his girlfriend, or he will have to go to the bathroom, or he'll be some pompous Frenchman who thinks your film would look best in the tricolors of the French flag. Meet your colorist before your transfer. If he is the type of guy you would like to go out and slug a few beers with, then he is probably right for you.

When you first walk into the colorist's suite, you will want to ask questions. Don't. Along with transferring film to video, the colorist will also write up a bill for the amount of time you spent in his room. Some guys are kind and will take off time for phone calls and excursions onto the Internet to check their fantasy football league. Then again, some will not. If you ask Mr. Colorist what that little button does and he launches into a fifteen-minute explanation, you might just have bought yourself the $125 answer. Save up all those questions for the end of the session. When the session is completed, deduct an hour from the amount of time you spent there and say to the colorist, "That was two hours, right?" He might say two and a half. Fine, you saved a half hour. You have also confirmed that you are off the clock. It is now safe to proceed with your question about that little button. The colorist will then share his views on the social and economic aspects of the most recent federal rate cut, as well as a myriad of war stories and other little tidbits designed to show you how important the people he works with are.

> *H I N T:* **Ask the posthouse if you can do your transfer at night. Rates usually come down when it gets into the small hours.**

OK, let's get back to the different equipment available for a film-to-tape transfer. There is another type of telecine made by Rank Cintel known as the URSA. One step up from that is the turbo URSA. A turbo works like this. Exhaust gas passes by a turbine as it is expelled from the engine. The more gas that passes by this turbine, the faster it spins. This turbine is connected to a spindle. On the other side (the engine's intake side) is another set of fan blades. As those blades spin faster and faster, they compress the engine's intake air into the car's cylinders. This is known as boost. The faster the blades spin, the more boost you have; the more boost you have, the more air is crammed into each cylinder. This extra air increases the force of the explosion created when the sparkplug ignites the gas-and-air mixture in the cylinder, and thus your car has more power. Why anybody would want to ram more air into a film-to-tape transfer machine is anybody's guess; perhaps it's just a gimmick by the manufacturer's marketing department.

Telecine machines are also made by Philips, Kodak, Sony—and the list goes on and on. Some people say these newer telecine machines will make 16 mm look like 35 mm. Not quite, but it will make your film look a little better. Like anything else in the film game, it will cost you. So pass on the supersize deluxe transfer and don't worry—it really wouldn't look like 35 mm anyhow. Also keep this in mind. You are doing this transfer to enable you to edit your film on video.

How Does One of These Machines Work?

Film creates a motion picture at 24 frames per second while video has 30 fps. How can you directly transfer something that is 24 to something that is 30? That doesn't add up, does it? Well, it does if you use something called **3:2 pulldown**. Remember that each frame of video is actually composed of two separate fields of video shown one right after the other; thus, video is being shown at 60 fields per second. If every frame of film were converted to 2 fields of video, you would come up with 48 fields of video—leaving you 12 short of a second. To make up those 12 fields, the Rank is going to take an extra video field from every other frame of film. This little trick will give you a grand total of 60 fields per second. That is how you stretch out 24 frames of film to fill 30 frames of video. That's all fine . . . until you have to sync up your sound.

Key Codes

Remember that you envisioned your film projected on a giant screen. Well, to keep that dream alive, you must have a special transfer done when you go to the lab and/or video house for your video transfer. The transfer employs **key codes** which are kind of like those little bar codes that are scanned at the checkout counter at the supermarket—only these run along the edge of the film every 20 frames in 16 mm.

How does the process work? While the lab is transferring your film to video, it is simultaneously making a copy to a three-quarter-inch U-Matic videotape, or any other format you wish. The lab is also burning a window on this copy that has a timecode matching your one-inch master. At the same time, a second window is being burned into the three-quarter-inch copy. This window contains the key code information.

Later on, after you win the state lottery, or open your door to find Ed McMahon standing on your porch with a five-foot cardboard check, you may have the opportunity to conform your negative and strike a print of your film. These codes can be taken off your video master and be used to pull the proper sections of film to cut your negative.

POP QUIZ **Which has key codes?**

Syncing Up Your Video Dailies

Posthouses also have the ability to sync up the sound to your picture as they make the video transfer. If you used a Nagra or DAT with timecode, then this service may be worthwhile. If not, it will add many hours to your transfer, enabling the owner of the post facility to get the BMW he has been eyeing. In fact, there are many people who would like you to buy them a BMW without your knowing it. So be cautious with your money. If you still have access to the Nagra or DAT, you may want to input the audio into your editing system and sync up the dailies yourself.

That sounds simple. So simple that it won't work.

Remember that video is actually running at 29.97 frames per second, not the 30 fps at which the telecine machine was running. That means your picture will be playing back at a slightly slower speed than it was recorded at. Your audio, however, will be playing back at exactly the same speed at which you recorded it. Because of this speed difference, your audio will slowly drift out of sync. This problem will be especially noticeable on longer takes. So what are you going to do about this problem? The labs have a special machine that slows down the tape to compensate for this problem, but you don't want to pay them one extra penny. Therefore, you are going to do a little preventative maintenance. Most DAT are recorded at a sample rate of 48 frames per second, the standard sampling rate for high-quality audio. But because you are smarter than everybody else in the world (and you have a friend who is a soundman), you record the dialogue onto the DAT at a sample rate of 48.048. When you play the DAT tape back at a sample rate of 48, you eliminate 0.1 percent. Now when you put the dialogue to the image, everything will stay in sync. This trick alone makes it well worth using a DAT instead of a Nagra. Remember that you're doing this because if and when you cut your negative and go to make a film print, you are going to have to bring the sound back to its original speed. This is known as **pull-up.**

Develop Normal and a One Lite Work Print (Editing on Film)

Don't do it. You have decided to edit your film on film. Sounds logical. It's not. Editing on film is messy. Things get lost. You have to rent a flatbed, an editing table for 16-mm film. Those things are the size of a couch and break down faster than you can say Fiat. Just stick to editing on video so I don't have to say, "I told you so."

If you have decided you are going to go back to the Stone Age of film editing, you probably will want to know what it's going to take to get the job done. We'll, I'll tell you, you insane lunatic. You're going to need a flatbed editing table, a few trim bins, and two cutting blocks (one straight, the other diagonal). When you take your film to the lab, have them make a one lite daily. Also, drop off your sound reels and have them transferred to fullcoat. Fullcoat is a magnetic recording medium identical in size and with the same sprocket-hole configuration as either 16- or 35-mm film. Once your sound is transferred to fullcoat it can remain in sync with your picture by mechanical means on a flatbed or upright editing table. Next, sync up the whole film, then drop it off at a place that does edge numbering—if you can find one. The technicians there are going to print little numbers on your film and fullcoat every 16 frames so you can log and check sync with this medieval version of timecode. Pick up your freakin' film, get some film cleaner and weable wipes, and start cutting.

That Guy in the Lab

Older gentlemen who have been in the industry for many years run film labs. They like to deal with large companies that are cash rich. Sure, they will take your film in and process it, but don't expect any special treatment. You will be given a number, and they will take their time developing your insignificant little film, giving preferred treatment to those they have done business with and gotten paid from in the past.

In a day or so, you will get a call from the lab informing you that your film is ready. If you have the money, go get it. If you don't, it's time to scrounge up the dough. A good place to start is the laundromat. With the right sized Allen wrench, it's a snap to pull out the agitator in any washing machine; and once inside, you will find all the change that was long ago given up for lost. Scoop up the dough and move on to the next laundromat. Eventually, you will return home and tell your mother, girlfriend, and anybody else who is willing to listen how excited you are because today you managed to find $26.12. That means you now only need $2,473.88 to get your film from the lab. Upon further explanation, you divulge that tomorrow you plan to visit the projects to plunder that Laundromat-rich area. At about this point, if anybody in your family truly cares about you and wishes to keep you from being incarcerated, a checkbook should materialize. Play the game to the end, complete with several "No, I couldn't possibly"s and then a smattering of the phrase "I insist"s; then move on to the endgame: "I'll pay you back."

Beware of the Techno-Sponging Know-It-Alls

When you least expect it, you will encounter one of these annoying individuals. You might run into him at the lab when you come to pick up or view your dailies. How will you know? Here is the classic warning sign: This guy will reel off a whole list of things that you should have done to make your picture that much better. These after-the-fact hints can be very annoying, especially when you don't know if your film is exposed properly, or if the soundman really did have the proper levels set.

Remember that the people on the fringe of the film industry at one time had the drive to make a film. One day, the economics of the situation forced them to take a job in the service industry. Their new reasoning goes like this: "So what if I have the lowly job of cleaning the toilet at the film lab, at least I'm still connected with the film industry." Your encounters with these film school graduates should motivate you. Remember, this could be you in three years. Better make a good film or call your broker and make sure you weren't invested in theglobe.com. (I was, and I couldn't make a film for a year and a half because of it.)

As you are living out this nightmare scenario, your newfound friend will feel an obligation to tell you his big fish story. He might tell you about how he was responsible for cutting the negative on the *Rocky and Bullwinkle Show,* or that he personally was responsible for watering and maintaining a certain celebrity's daffodils while he was in France filming a major studio motion picture. To this, respond with the standard "WOW!" and follow it up with "Oh crap, my meter just ran out and I can't afford to get my car towed." Then make tracks out the front door.

First Reaction

This is a very special time. Finally, you are seeing the fruits of your labor. Some of the shots that you thought would be great look like crap, and the ones that you thought were just so-so look great. The lighting isn't quite what you expected. The acting seems stiff. This is the raw material from which you will be building your film, so don't judge it too harshly. Take your video dailies and put them in a dark place so you don't destroy them when you return from your late night of crying and binge drinking.

Dailies are much like wine—they need to ferment. Put them out on the editing table and let them breathe for a day or so. When you return to them, they will have blossomed into something much better. OK, the truth is that you will have an understanding that you are stuck with the lighting that makes everybody look green and the walls pink and that there is not a damn thing you can do about the overacting that you didn't pick up on the set.

Editing

Cutting on Film

There once was a time when people actually touched film—and not only did they touch film, they cut it apart with a blade and then taped it together with a form of mutated Scotch tape that had little sprocket holes perforated down each side. This is how it used to be, be, be-eee-eee . . . ECHO.

A long time ago, in an editing room far, far away, there existed a machine called the flatbed. A **flatbed** is a table on which there were four to six circular objects known as plates. The center of the editing table has a projection system that casts your film's image onto a screen that is centered above the table. Below the optical system are two sound heads that pick up the audio from the full-coat and play it back through the system's speakers. Along the forward edge of the table are all kind of buttons, switches, knobs, and levers that control everything on the table either in unison or separately. If you are familiar with the controls that Captain Kirk and his gang used to fly the original *Enterprise* around in space, then you should be right at home using a flatbed editing table—the only thing missing is the colored blinking marbles and that weird earring that Spock sometimes wore. OK, let's edit.

The first step is to put your picture reel on the top left plate, then feed it through a maze of rollers and take it up on the opposing top plate. On the next plate, you would thread up a roll of magnetic tape called **fullcoat.** Fullcoat is the same size as 16-mm film and has sprocket holes along one edge. The surface is covered with magnetic media, thus the name fullcoat.

Once you had these two elements on their respective plates, you could hit the button for play and both sets of plates would be pulled through the machine in unison, the sprocket holes on both plates keeping everything in sync. A beam of light would shine through the picture and project it onto the little screen, while at the same point an audio head would pick up the audio signal on the fullcoat and play that back as well.

You would shuffle the thing along until you found the take you wanted to use. Then you would stop the thing and use a grease pencil to mark the spot on the film where you wanted to cut. At the same time, you would mark the fullcoat with a Sharpie.

Next, you would pull the film and fullcoat toward you and put them into a splicer and chop. Then you would make another chop on the other end at the last frame. The piece you just cut out you would hang in a bin, which was basically a trash can with little strips of metal running across the top that were covered with little wire tabs that you could hang the film from through a sprocket hole.

You would then tape the film back together and continue running the reel through the edit machine until you reached the next piece of film you wanted. Again you would chop, shuffle, chop, hang, and splice, and then you would move on to the next shot and start the process all over again. Once you had pulled out all the shots you wanted, you would take the reels off the machine and place them into boxes—one box for each sound and video reel. Next you would thread up some leader and, one by one, splice the shots hanging in the bin to the leader until all the pieces of film were connected. That was called the **assembly.**

You could play the assembly down and see how the shots selected work in juxtaposition with each other. Of course, you would need to find other shots or alternative takes, so you would have to take your assembly off the editing machine and put that into a box. Then, from your pile of boxes, you would pull the one that contained the new shot you were looking for. Then you would thread it up, shuffle through the roll, find the shot, hang up the shot, and put the assembly rolls back on shuffle up to the point you wanted to insert the new shot. Finally, amid the chop, chop, tape, "ouch," "$#@%ˆ$#@!" and "Damn blade," you would finish taping and hope for the best.

At that point you were saying to yourself, "There has to be a better way."

Editing Deck to Deck

In the beginning of the video revolution, three things were invented: the video camera, the video deck, and the balding guy with a large cranium who knew how to fix all this stuff when it overheated. I'm not sure of the order in which they were created. It's a question of which came first? The chicken or the egghead?

A video editing system at its most basic is comprised of two video decks and a little console known as a **controller** that allows the editor to tell the decks what to do. The decks are known as the **playback deck** and the **record deck,** and they do just what their names suggest. One deck will play back the source material, while the other will record the sections you have selected at the desired time.

The most basic edit controller is called an RM-450 and is made by Sony. If you can work it, you could probably work any of the clones created by the other electronic giants. An edit controller usually has a bunch of buttons that mimic those on video decks. These are just duplicates that allow you to control the deck without leaning over and hitting the button on the deck's faceplate. The buttons on the left side of the controller are for the playback deck and are usually labeled as such, while those on the right are for controlling the record deck. Also, there is usually a shuttle knob that gives you variable speed control to scan through your footage as fast as the tape transport can go, or as slowly as frame by frame.

The first step is to pop a new tape into the record deck and feed it black from another little box called a **black burst generator** and hit the record button. This is called **striping the tape**, and it is very important. As the deck records black onto the video tracks, it is also laying down something called an address track.

The **address track** is a reference track that the edit controller and the deck will utilize during the editing process to enable them to find specific points on the tape. It creates, as its name implies, an address for every video frame on the tape.

Once the tape is blacked and striped with the address track, it is time to start editing. The other most crucial buttons on the edit controller are marked EDIT IN (or IN POINT) and EDIT OUT (or OUT POINT) or anything else that closely resembles these words. First you are going to shuffle about a minute forward on the tape in the record deck. Once you reach that point, you are going to hit the IN button on the controller. This places the address track information for the point where the record deck is stopped into the edit controller's memory.

The next step is to select the first shots to edit together. Find the tape and throw it into the playback deck again, shuffle forward until you find the exact frame you wish to start with, stop the deck, and hit the IN button on the controller. Move forward to the last frame you wish to include from this shot. Stop on the frame and hit the OUT button. There is no need to use the OUT button on the record side because it will stop automatically after the playback deck reaches its out point. We have now programmed the edit controller to perform and edit; the only thing left to do is to actually execute it.

Look at the middle of the controller; there will be two large buttons, one marked EDIT and the other PREVIEW. The PREVIEW button will perform the edit but not actually record it to tape, while the EDIT button will commit itself to the rearrangement of metallic oxide, thus editing your video. Be brave; go ahead and hit the EDIT button. Both decks should immediately snap into motion. They will find the point on each tape you have selected, pause, and then rewind for exactly five seconds. They will then both roll forward in unison to the point you marked. The electric signal will flow from the playback deck to the record deck, and the shot you have just selected will be recorded onto the tape. Now all you do is select your next shot, mark the in point on the record deck and the in and out points on the playback deck, and hit the RECORD button. Repeat this over and over and you will have completed the first assembly of your film—well, kind of.

Here is the rub of machine-to-machine video editing. In short, it is a linear process. Say the first shot in your movie is the giant explosion; the second, the guy with the really big gun. You then move forward and edit the remainder of your movie. Each new shot will pick up against the last frame of the shot that precedes it. You will line up shots in this manner until . . . well, until you change your mind. And being a member of the human race you will change your mind—that is certain.

As you finish reading your favorite periodical and reach for the flusher, you will pause—and realize that you have a new solution that just might make the beginning of your movie a little more palatable. You originally opened your movie with a shot of the giant exploding sun, followed by the guy with the really big gun. But now you realize that the alien with the rocket-propelled grenade launcher should be the second shot, and the third shot should be the guy with the big gun. Well, if you want to put the new second shot in, you would have to push every shot that comes after it back by the same amount of time. But you can't just push these shots back without actually rerecording them into their new position on the master tape. To do this, you have to find each and every shot and reedit them in after the new shot of the alien with the rocket-propelled grenade. Another solution is to start a whole new tape. You could then record the first shot followed by your new second shot. Then you would place the old edit tape in the playback deck and let the whole sequence from the second shot down to the end record in as one big chunk. The drawback here is video quality. Every time you rerecord a segment, it loses a generation in quality. After about six or seven generations, your video quality quickly deteriorates to that of a videophone call from Mom.

As you are looking at several flesh-colored smudges and contemplating yet another option for the middle of your film, you might find yourself saying, "If only there was a way I could magically drop a shot into the middle of two other shots and have everything shift down the appropriate number of frames so I don't need to keep rerecording chunks of my film over and over again." And this brings us to the third and best editing solution.

Nonlinear Editing

Today, the editing systems of choice are computer-based nonlinear edit systems. These systems are now the norm in all aspects of film production. Just as the name implies, these systems run on a computer platform—either a PC or an Apple, depending on the supplier you choose. Let's take a quick look at the systems that are available today and what they mean to you, the extremely poor and getting-poorer-every-day filmmaker.

Avid is like the Kleenex and Frisbee of the nonlinear editing world. A lot of people will say they are editing on an Avid even though they might be editing on a competitor's system. Avid systems have been around the longest, which has allowed them to increase the features and stability of the system. In the beginning, Avid was based on the Apple operating system, but several years ago, when it looked like Apple might not last, Avid migrated to Windows NT. Avid systems now operate in both environments. Avid is a very good choice for a nonlinear system, but just like Bounty, the quicker picker-upper, you are going to pay a premium for the name. Avid also has lower-end machines that are somewhat limited in features but are a lot more appealing to the wallet.

Media 100 is another system you may encounter. Like Avid, Media 100 has systems available for both PC and Apple platforms. Media 100 has a price point below that of Avid while maintaining comparable features. Both Avid and Media 100 are hardware- and software-based editing solutions. This means that you will need to install a variety of computer cards into the PCI slots in your computer as well as load in the software. That will allow your computer to utilize these specialized boards.

Next up is **Final Cut Pro,** a system that is both a software and a software-hardware solution. If you have shot on digital video and your camera and computer both have a firewire interface, you can input your footage, edit, and then output your footage back to the camera without coughing up cash for a capture card. If you don't have firewire capabilities, then you will have to buy a capture card compatible with both your computer and Final Cut Pro. These range from a couple of hundred dollars to almost $10,000, depending on the features and quality of video you desire. Final Cut Pro is definitely the up-and-coming-cool-guy system that you might want to give some serious consideration.

Finally, there is Adobe Premiere, a software editing solution that has been around for many years—and every year it gets easier and easier to operate. However, its interface tends to be somewhat confusing, and its features are limited and sometimes time consuming. That said, you might just have a copy of it that came bundled with some other software, and that would make the price right, wouldn't it?

Those four are the most prevalent systems you will come across as of today, January 12, 2002, at 4:02 Eastern Standard Time. Tomorrow, all bets are off. Sure there are many other systems out there—Edit, Plum, Purple, and Razor—but you can bet that before you can read this sentence one of these companies will be bought by another and have its system renamed or integrated into another brand. The good news is that all these systems operate in the same basic way.

How Do I Work This Crazy Thing? (Or, How an Avid and All Its Competitors Work)

The first step in computer-based nonlinear editing is something called **digitization.** The process works like this. You first connect your video deck to your computer on higher-end systems, using something called a **breakout box.** This will have a group of BNC, RCA, and XLR connectors in two groups—one for input and the other for output. This box will be connected to the computer card that came along with the video editing system. Low-end systems will have a cable with BNC and RCA connectors that will also lead back to the video card that came bundled with the editing system. Either way, find the appropriate cables and hook one end up to the video deck and the other end to the input of the breakout box or the cable. Next, turn to the computer screen. Somewhere in the menu there will be an option called DIGITIZE; go ahead and select that. Next you hit play on the deck, and as soon as you see the first frame you wish to capture, you hit the CAPTURE button on your computer screen.

The hard drive on your computer will immediately swing into high gear. As the video information flows into the computer, it is encoded into digital data and stored on your hard drive. At the same time, your computer is reading the timecode of the tape so it will have a frame-accurate reference to the original videotape. At the end of the tape, you will hit STOP. The computer will then compare the timecode from the first frame of video it captured to the timecode of the last frame captured from the video deck. It will count how many frames of video it captured and then interpolate what the timecode should be on the last frame of video it captured. If these numbers match, everything is fine and you can move on to digitizing the next tape.

If they don't match, you have to find out why and remedy the situation before you continue. The usual culprit is you—you checked the tape on location and left an empty space in the middle of it. While you still will be able to edit later on, when you need to go back to your original tapes, the reference will not be accurate, and the computer will place the wrong piece of video into your program. Take care to do it right from the start, because fixing it later will take many long nights accompanied by a long string of epithets.

As you digitize each tape into the computer, it will be stored as a graphical representation known as a **clip.** You can name the clip so it will have some meaning for you and select a frame from the video to be shown when you pull up the clip. These clips are grouped together into windows on your computer called **bins.** Again, you can name the bins and sort clips into different bins by category. For example, one bin could be called "sunset," and in that bin you would have only shots of clowns—oops, right, in that bin you would only have shots of sunsets.

Now that you have all your footage digitized into the computer's hard drive, it's time to edit. When you edit your film, the picture and sound will be played back from these hard drives. When you double-click on a clip, it is instantly brought into the playback window. You can play this clip down at normal speed or you can scan through it at one hundred times the normal speed until you get to the point you wish to use. You can also instantly skip to the very end of the clip without scanning through its entirety. All this is done instantly, making shots available to edit as fast as you can click your mouse.

You will construct a program, or timeline. This is a graphical representation of your movie. A short shot will be a small box in your timeline; a longer shot will be a longer rectangle. The timeline tells the computer where on the hard drive to find the footage that is to be played back. The computer will then jump back and forth to the hard drive, playing back the footage in the order dictated in the program. Your video is never actually cut, just accessed in the order you dictated. Therefore, it is known as nonlinear editing.

Remember the problems of deck-to-deck film editing when you want to insert a new shot into the beginning of the film after you had edited together thirty minutes of footage. In the nonlinear world, this is a no-brainer. You can grab all the clips after the shot you wish to change and simply drag them away from the opening shots, thus creating a gap in your timeline. You will then drag the new shot into this. If you want a longer shot, you can make the gap bigger; if you decide the shot needs to be shorter, you can do this as well. Then you can drag all the shots that precede it back to the right so they butt up against the last frame of the new shot. This is the power of nonlinear editing systems. It also gives you the ability to save an unlimited number of versions of your edit, all instantly available for playback and comparison.

The Free Lesson

Now that you know the basic theory behind nonlinear editing, it's time to get a little hands-on experience. Find out the name of the dealer who sells the editing system you are most interested in using. Give the dealer a call and tell the sales rep that you are thinking about purchasing a couple of machines to replace the old toaster you have been using. Be sure to mention you are unsure about what system to buy but have narrowed it down between the one he sells and another he doesn't. The next part is easy: Sit back and let him talk. Eventually, he will invite you to a demonstration he is holding at the local Marriott. Bingo! You just got yourself a lesson. When you attend, be sure to ask lots of question about the machine and enjoy all the cheese plates and free soda. Now, you may have gotten some pretty good information from this group demonstration, but you and I know nothing is better then a little one-on-one tutoring. With this in mind, you are on to phase two of your plan.

After the demo, notify the salesman that you are worried that the interface you just looked at seems rather complicated. The salesman will now invite you to come back to the shop for a one-on-one session so he can show you how user-friendly his system is. This is called a **free lesson.** The more interested you are in a competitor's system, the more free lessons you can get.

(A word to all nonlinear editing manufacturers: The name Avid is just a search and replace away from extinction in this book if you would like to supply the author with a demo system of your clearly superior product. Well, let's just say I'm ready to use some of the more advanced features on this word processing program.)

Syncing It Up

If you shot on film instead of video, welcome to syncland. Before you can edit frame one, you are going to have to sync up your film dailies. For those of you who shot on video, go directly to the "Logging and Log Sheets" section later in this chapter.

If you chose to fly in the face of convention and are editing on film, using a flatbed, the sync-up process goes like this. First you will place your picture and corresponding audio rolls onto your flatbed. Scan down until you find the first shot you wish to sync up; find the first frame on which you can see the slate clearly closed; mark this frame. Then, using a Sharpie, mark an X on the corresponding audio frame. Remember that you will always have more audio than picture, so shuffle forward until you hear the sound of the slate closing on your audio track. Mark this frame of audio with an X as well. Now place this second X to the right of the blade on the editing block. Pull the sound tape from the take-up side until you find the first X and lay it over the second X. Chop the fullcoat and pull out the excess, then splice the two pieces of film together. That's it; the shot is now in sync.

Work your way through the roll in this manner, then put some white leader on the end of each roll. You should place a mark on the tail leader of the sound and picture so you can sync them up from the back of the roll. If you encounter huge amounts of picture that was shot MOS (that means without sound), you are going to need **fill leader** to fill in the void on your audio track. Fill leader is actually a print of somebody's film that was no good; but because it is a print, there are only sprocket holes on one side. You can splice it into your audio track to fill up space and not worry about the sprockets flying over the sound head, making all kinds of weird noises and actually wearing down the head in the process.

Syncing It Up on a Deck-to-Deck Edit System

Load your first picture tape into the record deck; your first sound tape goes into the playback deck. Shuttle your record deck forward until you find the very first frame on which the slate appears closed. Mark this as your in point on the record deck. Now shuffle your sound deck forward and listen for the call numbers that match up with those that are on the slate. When you find them, slowly jog forward until you hear the sound of the slate. Find the very first frame on which you can hear the clap. Mark this as your in point on the playback deck.

> *WARNING:* **Make sure the editing system is on INSERT EDIT and audio tracks one and two are punched up. Do not edit the picture.**

Press the preview button and see what happens. If the lips match the voice, then you are in sync. Press the PERFORM button and lay the sound over. Continue this process until all your sound takes are synced up. Make sure you never shuttle forward on your sound tape. Always look for picture, not sound.

Syncing It Up
on a Nonlinear
Edit System

Syncing up your film on a nonlinear edit system is quite simple. This is a basic strategy that will work for all systems, but bear in mind that the name of the function might vary from manufacturer to manufacturer. Still, you should be able to do the translation (after all, you are a filmmaker and nothing can stand in your way). First, create a timeline and drag your first reel of picture into it. With the mouse, you should be able to scan through the picture. Do so until you find the first frame on which the slate is closed. Mark this frame. Then pull up your audio. Listen until you hear the first frame of the slate clapping. Mark this frame as the in point in the edit suite window. Drag this audio into the timeline, lining up the first frame of the audio with your marked frame of the slate closing. Release the mouse, and the audio will drop into the timeline. You are now in sync.

Logging and Log
Sheets

As you sync up your footage, it is important to make log sheets that have all the timecode numbers. Write down the timecode numbers that coincide with the closed slate on the picture track and the sound of the slate on the audiotape. You also should jot down the scene number of the take and a brief description of the scene. These notes are important; they will help you find shots you need in the editing process, so make them neat. The other crucial thing to place in your logbook is a section for general comments like "This shot sucks" or "Can use the end only." Later, when you are searching for a shot to save a scene, these notes may jar your memory and the solution to an editing nightmare could fall into your lap. One more thing about your logbook; I call it inspiration. Every time you look at this book you want something to inspire you to make your movie the best it can be. So find an image that speaks to you and paste it onto the logbook's cover. I know it sounds a little sentimental, but just do it—and save your skepticism for the late-night infomercials.

Editing Theory

Now that you know what technology is available to help you edit your film, it's time to talk about editing technique. Editing is an art form, just like lighting, screenwriting, and directing. Some are born with the skill. Other learn it over many years by apprenticing with top editors in the field, and a few pick it up overnight by reading a few run-on sentences strung together in a film book. Whatever the case, ladies and gentlemen, let's start editing.

The theory behind editing is very simple. When you cut from the wide shot to a close-up of your actor, you want his face to be pointing in roughly the same direction. If his hands match, you are so much better off. This is called **match cutting.** The action from the first shot to the second shot is continued. The closer the action matches, the better the cut. Once you start cutting, you will begin to understand the importance of continuity. When the actor picks up the glass with his right hand in the wide shot and then uses his left hand in the close-up, you're quickly going to come to the realization that you might not be able to cut the two shots together. It is at this point that you will curse the actor for having used the wrong hand; you may even be tempted to relegate his headshot to the trusty old dartboard for further punishment. At this point, it would be wise not to do anything brash, especially because you may need this actor again to record some key lines or to reshoot a shot that came out completely black.

OK, back to editing. The thing to remember about editing is that it should be invisible. You want to manipulate your audience to see what is important, but you don't want them to realize what you're doing. On a purely mechanical level, it never hurts to cut on a motion. For example, when your character pulls out his Uzi, you might want to cut out of your wide shot as the gun moves out of his coat. Then you might cut to the medium shot of that character picking up the gun as it moves up and levels off. The action of the raising gun will attract your audience's attention; it will fix its attention on this, and your cut will go by unnoticed. Keep this in mind while editing.

OK, your actor picks up the gun with his left hand in the wide shot, but he uses his right in the dolly shot that you are definitely using because it took three hours to set up. Again, there is a way out. After the wide shot, cut to the bad guys, then cut back to the dolly shot. The audience will never know that the gun switched hands. They are stupid. Trust me.

Enough theory; let's get our hands dirty. Fire up the editing system, take your seat at the helm, and start editing. Put in the first shot and move forward. Don't be afraid to try new things. After about an hour of editing a scene that is giving you a little trouble, you are going to say, "How friggin' obvious! I should have shot it that way with a close-up and a dolly shot." By editing your film, you are going to learn more about directing than you ever imagined. This is a very powerful argument for editing your own film. Once you cut two shots together that don't work no matter what you do, you will quickly realize that perhaps you should have listened to the DP on this one and moved the camera to a slightly different angle, but you didn't because you were in a rush and the DP was getting on your nerves that day.

Ping-Pong Cutting

This is one of the hallmarks of a first-time editor. Ping-Pong cutting goes like this. Every time a character has a line of dialogue you will cut to them saying it. You will then cut back to the character with the next line. And so it will go throughout the entire scene—back and forth, back and forth. Remember that you are working in a visual medium, and sometimes you can learn a lot about a person from his or her reaction. Remember the little directing tip about having actors look away from and then back at the character who is speaking? Well, this is when all those lookups, lookovers, and look-aways come into play. The only way to see these reactions in a film is if you cut them in as some other character is talking. The looks toward, away, or down just make it that much easier to get your message across. If you cut in a lookaway, it will show the character is disinterested; a look toward will show interest. Basically, find the proper look for the message you are trying to convey from this character. However, I would not cut away from the character as he is speaking his last line. I think it's important to show the characters on screen for their last lines of dialogue.

Jump Cuts

A jump cut purposely mismatches the action when cutting from one shot to another. This can be effective when it is done for effect, to draw the audience's attention to something. Jump cuts can also be integrated into the overall editing style of the movie. The danger of jump cuts is using them as an excuse for bad film-making. The film *Breathless* (not the one with Richard Gere) was one of the first films to use jump cuts as part of its visual style; take a look at it and decide for yourself if jump cuts are for you.

MTV Cutting

Quick cuts, crazy camera angles, weird lighting effects, guys with long hair, and slutty girls. All these things look great when they are cut to music. However, the idea here is for people to understand your movie, not throw up because of motion sickness. So don't be tempted to do the MTV cutting thing.

Rearrange Scenes

On the first pass or assembly of your movie, you should keep faithful to the script. Arrange the scenes in the order they were intended, and then see how they play together. After you screen this first cut, you can then try shuffling scenes. You will be surprised how often a scene that is moved around can help clarify the story for the audience. Don't go shuffling the deck randomly; but if you think a scene might play better somewhere else, give it a try.

A big part of editing is trial and error. So what if it doesn't work? You can just move it back again. Another thing you can do is borrow a shot from another scene. Say you need a close-up of your main character looking left, but you didn't shoot the scene that way. You might be able to find the shot in the dailies for another scene and use it. The thing that will usually trip you up here will be the lighting; if it doesn't even remotely match, your audience will sense the cheat.

Temp Track

Many editors find it useful to edit to some kind of music. This is called a **temp track** because it is only for your own use as the film editor. This means that you can choose any music in the world to edit to. So go ahead, buy a bunch of CDs (they're now a tax write-off). Then place the music into your film and see how it affects the mood and tone of the piece you are cutting. You might have to go through several selections to find the musical piece that is right for the scene you are cutting, so don't fall in love with the first piece of music you try. Also keep in mind that you are building up a music track that would take a major coup in Vegas to pay for. This is a temp track, and the word *temp* means temporary while you edit.

Computer Meltdowns—How to Deal

One morning, you are going to enter the edit suite, fire up the machine, and be greeted by a bunch of empty bins. It will be just as if all your shots just disappeared into thin air. But you know better—you are experiencing a computer crash.

We have all lost important data on our computers. Maybe you have had a crash while you have been writing a manuscript for a how-to book and lost five pages, or maybe your accounting program has crashed, forcing you to reinput last month's bank deposits. But nothing can prepare you for the pure terror that accompanies a possible loss of data on a nonlinear editing system.

A crash *will* happen to you, but the key here is to remain calm. Computers fail in nonlinear edit systems. The most common failures are the high-speed hard drives that hold the video and audio media. Don't upgrade, don't downgrade, don't do anything while you are in the middle of a project. Don't throw away any data or media because you're sure you won't be needing it later. Don't defrag your hard drive or update your operating system. About 99.97 percent of computer malfunctions are caused by something you have done.

If the computer starts acting wacky, think about the last thing you did. Maybe you moved a file to a new area, or maybe you just finished digitizing a piece of media. The first step in undoing a computer problem is to bring the machine back to the state it was in when everything was working properly. If you just brought in a piece of media and things start going haywire, throw it away. If the media didn't digitize properly, it may be corrupt. This could cause your machine to crash. If you moved a file around, the machine might be looking for it; again, this may cause the machine to crash. Usually this first step will solve the problem.

If none of that helps, check all the connectors; a loose one can cause mayhem. It is also a good idea to check all the pins in the SCSI connectors, because if one is slightly bent or not making contact it could be responsible for your newfound headache. Listen to the sounds your machine is making. A bad hard drive will sound different from a working one. Another clue is the little lights—these may blink differently than usual when the drive has gone bad. If it's the hard drive, you will have to redigitize the show. It's not the end of the world—just an annoying, time-consuming process.

If all else fails and you still have technical support, you may want to give it a shot. Just remember the golden rule: The guy on the other end of the phone might not know as much as you think. If your gut tells you the tech guy is not making sense, end the phone call. Call back, and maybe the next guy can get you through the situation. This may take a couple of tries and a few rolls of antacid. In the end, it may be to your benefit to try to solve the problem yourself. I have found that the best way to do this is to hit the road, get away from the computer, and take a drive or a jog or go for one of the juice drinks—just get away from that computer. As you suck down a carrot, beet, and apple concoction, you might just have an epiphany. Finish your drink and head back to the computer to try out your new revelation.

Titles

Titles are very often the first thing an audience will see when they sit down at the theater or in your living room to view the first cut of your film. Remember that you only get to make a first impression once, so your titles are very important. Your titles should have a feel. They should prepare the audience for the film that is going to follow them. They should be suspenseful and interesting, perhaps even moody. Your film should dictate the feel of your title sequence.

I can usually tell from an opening title sequence if I will like a film. Try it. Go to the movies. After the opening title sequence ends, judge the movie just on the basis of typefaces, font serifs, and the visuals behind them. Chances are that if you liked the titles, you will like the movie. Conversely, if you didn't care for the zany animated sequence, you will probably be disappointed with the film that follows.

The cheapest and fastest way to shoot titles is to do it on set. This usually works best when you decide on some highly stylized motif that will reinforce your film's visual style. If your film takes place at a coffee shop, you could write each title in black magic marker on a cup and then shoot each cup with a different background within the coffee-shop set. If you insist on white titles over a black background, you can always print them up on your computer.

Of course, you could always use the character generator that comes bundled with your editing solution of choice. This is a valid tool. But for some reason, these computer-generated letters always seem a little jarring to me. You could call this an issue of personal taste, but I do not like the look or feel of computer-generated titles. I would rather scribble the titles on a napkin and film that.

End Credits

Your end titles are a great opportunity to get a little humor into your film. Although only five people have worked on your film, your credits will consist of hundreds of names and an equal number of jobs. Don't be afraid to put stupid, useless information into your titles. People love that kind of stuff. Don't forget to throw in the names of those who bought a credit. At the very end, include the word *copyright,* the year, and your name. You might also want to take this opportunity to use some of those hilarious outtakes; a liberal sprinkling of those throughout the titles is also a valid way to increase the running time of your film.

Adobe After Effects

Today, title sequences are becoming more and more elaborate. It started a few years back with the movie *Seven*. The good news for you is that this opening sequence was created with a computer program that is readily available now, known as Adobe After Effects. The bad news is this program is rather confusing. The even better news: Once you get the hang of it, you can make an amazing title sequence, output it to film, and then dazzle your audience just like the big guys.

FILMLOOK

Yes, there is actually a process you can apply to your finished video project that will make the image appear as if it were shot on film. This is known as **FILMLOOK**. FILMLOOK works by introducing a number of filmlike qualities into the video image. It adds grain and changes the color and black level to mimic the qualities of film. In addition, it changes the frame rate to mimic that of a film-to-video transfer. The lab cost is usually minimal, or you could go out and buy the software yourself.

Will I Lose My Girlfriend?

You might. A strange thing happens to the human body while it is editing. All your sexual desires are thrown into the background. You will find yourself thinking about two things: The first is what shot you should use in a particular scene; the second is food. At first you will be content to gorge out on Twinkies and Ho-Hos. You will then progress to the eat healthy phase. You will go out of your way to avoid junk food and bologna. During this phase, you will eat an ungodly amount of tuna fish and wash it down with seltzer water. One day you will go to the deli to pick up your tuna sandwich and *bang!* It will happen—you will enter phase three. You will find yourself becoming impatient as the little lady in front of you in line, who must be a hundred years old and is shrinking before your very eyes, searches her ridiculously small purse for exact change.

There is no turning back now that you are in stage three, otherwise known as *the big rush*. You will find yourself moving extremely rapidly for no apparent reason. Days will begin to melt into night, and vice versa. This means your film is almost done. You will eat anything as long as it can be made in less than thirty seconds. Finally, you will awaken one morning in an empty apartment. Empty, that is, except for that scrap of paper pinned to the front door. A note. It reads: "I have left you and your stupid film. Don't try to find me. I have run off with the guy downstairs to design custom jewelry for a New Age shop in Bohemia—hope you and your film have a nice life together."

Take a Vacation

Get away from your film for a couple of days. Climb a mountaintop and yell out your name. Go swim the English Channel. Just get away. You have been living, dreaming, eating, and crapping your film for the last six months; the chances of your being objective while viewing your film are about the same as getting bitten by a shark off the Florida coast during August in the year 2001—possible, but not likely. You are going to give yourself some distance from your film, so when you return to the editing room, you will have the proper perspective to decide between the cyanide pill and reading the next couple of chapters in this book.

The First Screening

You should come back to your film fresh and ready to make the final cut. First, screen your film. No, not alone. You now have to make sure the story is working. No, you can't judge the story yourself. *Why?* You understand it, of course. After all, you wrote the goddamn thing. You need an impartial audience. So get a couple of opinionated friends over. Pick the ones who are not afraid to hurt your feelings. Yes, you might have to spring for the beer. Set them up in front of the TV and let it rip.

As your acquaintances view the film, you should make a list of cuts that do not work and things you might want to change. When the lights come on, pass out some questionnaires.

Sample Questionnaire

What was the story about?
Did you understand the story?
What did you like the least?
What did you like the best?
What is your good-looking sister's phone number?
Would you pay money to see this movie?
If you answered yes to the last question, can you give me some money for the beer?

After you collect the papers, have a discussion. Ask your friends what they think. For a couple of minutes, you will watch their blank faces. Now it's time to swing into action. Prod and probe everybody for all the information you can get; it's your turn to play the part of the Gestapo, so relish it. All this information will be crucial to you as you make the final cut.

Reshoots and Pickups

After the screening, you will be peppered with ideas and suggestions from well-meaning people who don't really understand the amount of pain and suffering that has transpired to get your film to this point. But in every group of film critics, one person is liable to suggest adding a scene to clarify something about a character's childhood, making it easier to understand why he finds himself staring at a windmill for three hours every day.

If you were to take this person's suggestion and add an entirely new scene, that would be called a **pickup.** If you were to alter an existing scene and film the character explaining his attraction to windmills and insert these new lines into the edited version of your film, it would be called a **reshoot.**

Whether you want to call it a pickup or a reshoot, both entail a monumental effort on your part. I'm not saying it's a bad thing, I'm just saying you should sleep on it before plunging forward into the land of pickups and reshoots. Now think back to the last day of shooting. Think hard now. Did you tell anybody to jump off a cliff who you now need in order to shoot additional scenes? Pray you were kind.

The Fine Cut

This is the end. Make another pass through your movie. This final pass will take care of any bad cuts that managed to slip through up to this point. Along the way, fix scenes. Maybe rearrange a few to help people understand the story. You will try to fix any bad cuts and fine-tune the ones that are close but not quite right. You may need to cut a couple of frames here and there. Also, edit in any reshoots, insert the main titles into the film's beginning, and tag on the end credits.

Online Cut

You have completed your film, and I mean *completed*. It's done. The truth of the matter is that you could keep working on it forever. So you're going to have to be strong. Stick to your guns and say, "I will not try to change my cut unless I have a really great, and I mean great, idea." Say this over and over, and maybe you can limit yourself to one more set of revisions before your film gets to a point where it would be totally unfeasible economically to make a change.

Welcome to the endgame. The big decision here is whether to finish the film on film or to finish it on video. Anybody who screens your film is going to request a VHS copy. In order to make a good-quality VHS tape, you are going to need a video master. Producing a video master is much simpler and cheaper than producing a print of your finished film. This means that for now you will finish your film on video. This brings us to something called an online. An **online** is the process of reconstructing your film from the original high-quality masters and editing them together onto a high quality video format like Digital Betacam.

There are two ways you can online your film—both will produce a high-quality master, and there is only one way you can make a print of your film. Yes, yes, I'll tell you how. Just keep reading.

Nonlinear Online

The process here is quite simple. You are going to replace the low-resolution dailies with a high-resolution video of just the shots or portion of shots used in your final cut of the movie. This is known as redigitization (or redigi, for short).

First, select all the clips that are in your timeline. Next, there should be a menu item somewhere that reads *batch digitization*, go ahead and select that. Now you are going to change the resolution rate to one that is online quality. This can be expressed as a data rate, in which case you would want to select one in the neighborhood of 150 kilobytes (KB) per frame, or it just might be in plain English and read as online or something similar. Next, the computer will ask you to place a tape into the video deck. It will then scan through the tape, only digitizing the portions in your final cut at a very high data rate onto the computer's hard drives. You will go through your master tapes one by one until you have reassembled the completed picture in high resolution. You can now master this high-resolution version of your film to Beta SP or any other high-quality video format.

Linear Online

The same process can be completed in a deck-to-deck edit suite. If you edited on a nonlinear system, you can produce an **edit decision list** (EDL). If you edited deck to deck, you will have to manually write down the timecode numbers at the first and last frame of every shot. Also, lay down your cut on a tape so you have a visual reference. Either way, you will then go to a posthouse and either load in your EDL from the disk or manually type it into the edit controller. You will then rebuild your film from the original videotapes shot by shot. As you do this, you will also rebuild the dialogue track onto the master tape you are now producing.

The Negative Cut and the Negative Cutter

The reason for cutting the film's negative is so you can make a print. After all, that is why you got into this business in the first place. To project your work. The process goes like this.

Once you have completed your film, you will output a video copy of it from the editing system you chose to cut your film on. The edit decision list is stored in something called the **CMX 3400 format.** The only purpose here is to save your list in a format that almost anybody can read, and the CMX 3400 format is just that.

Now you are going to pack up all your original camera negatives, all the original video transfer tapes, the edit list, and the VHS copy of your movie, and hand that over to the negative cutter. He is going to go through each original roll of negative and input the timecode and key code numbers into a computer. He then enters your EDL into the same computer. This computer will spit out a list of shots he needs to cut from your original negative and string together to make your negative match the edited version of your movie.

Now we all know that computers screw up, so to double-check that this doesn't happen, he will visually compare the first frame of each shot with the VHS editing copy of the film you have provided him. Once he or she has cut out all the shots from your original negative, the cutter will string them together into something called an **AB roll.**

The cutter actually makes two rolls of film: one represented by the letter A the other by the letter B. The first shot on roll A will be the first shot of your film. Opposite this shot on the B roll will be black leader that will run the exact length to the frame of the first shot on the A roll. The second shot will be placed at the end of this black leader on the B roll. And so it will go, back and forth, until all your shots are placed in order, alternating between the A and the B rolls.

The reason for this has to do with the way film is spliced together. When your negative is cut, it is reassembled by actually gluing it back together. To get the glue to stick to the film, the emulsion has to be scraped off the edge of the film. The glue is then applied to this strip, which is stuck to the black leader. But when the emulsion is scraped off, it just leaves a clear area. If this were glued directly to another shot and not the black leader, you would see a white line at the top of every frame when a shot switches in the print. This would be very distracting. By alternating from the A and B rolls and splicing the film to black leader, you are hiding this white line. That is the reason for A and B rolling the negative cut.

The Zero Cut

This sounds rather mysterious, and it is. When your negative cutter splices two shots together, he is actually going to take a pair of scissors and cut your negative halfway through the frame in front of the first one he needs and after the last one he needs at the end of the shot. This frame is now destroyed. Now say you had a shot that was 24 frames long, and you wanted to use the first 12 frames in one scene and the last 12 frames in another. When your negative cutter pulls the first sequence, he is going to cut through your film on frame 13, which is also the first frame of the second 12-frame sequence. He has just done a zero cut. To avoid this you need to skip at least a frame—and preferably two—when you split up a take to use in two different areas of your movie.

The Answer Print

Next, you will drop off your A and B rolls along with your sound mix at the lab. You will instruct the lab to make a **married first-answer print.** The lab will quickly swing into action. Your audio mix will go to the lab's sound department; there the technicians will make something known as an **optical track.** That's the squiggly line that runs along the edge of your film. Remember those films about frogs you saw in junior high school? Yup, the white line that ran along one side of the film, was the optical track. A light shining though it, called an **exciter lamp,** transfers this meaningless line into sound.

Meanwhile, a colorist will be looking through your film, shot by shot, on a machine called a **hazeltine.** He or she is going to input how much red, green, and blue light the printing machine should shine through your negative. The purpose: to make sure the color balance of the film will match from shot to shot. Once the colorist is done, he or she will run your A and B rolls and the optical track through a printing machine, marrying all these elements together onto one strip of film that will be now known as your **first answer print.**

It is called an answer print because the lab is not going to make any other prints until they get an answer from you saying that you are satisfied with the print. Most often, you will have a gripe with the way the colorist has colored a scene. At this point, you will have a meeting with him and tell him that yes, you wanted the oranges to be purple because that is a symbol of bravery in the Sudanese military. He will go back and change the oranges to purple, and the lab will reprint your film. Now you have something known as the **second answer print.** Again the lab is waiting for your answer. By this time you are broke, so you will most likely accept whatever they have given you.

When you screen an answer print, you should also listen to the sound very carefully. In short, sound on 16-mm film goes from bad to horrible. You want to make sure you are getting at the very least very bad to bad sound, but you will not settle for sound in the horrible-to-dismal range.

Sound

ou now hold in your hand an edited master of your film that contains only the location dialogue on the audio track. Feels pretty damn good, doesn't it? Enjoy the moment, because plenty of work lies ahead.

Sound is very important. And if you don't get it recorded right on the set or on location, it will cost you a lot of time and money in postproduction to fix it. So don't tell the sound guy to go to hell when he is having trouble; take a minute and work it out. Nothing screams out _amateur production_ more than a bad sound track (and I'm not talking music). If the people in the audience cannot hear what your characters are saying, they will quickly become frustrated. For some reason an audience can get past dark, grainy images and even the occasional out-of-focus shot, but throw in a couple of undecipherable lines of dialogue and you are screwed. Fortunately for you, the audio you recorded on the set is only the basis for your final sound track. You will take this raw material and carefully sculpt and mold it into a world-class sound track that would make any parent proud. In order to start your journey to a better sound track, it's important you understand the processes that are available. Let's take a look at how a big-budget movie with unlimited resources goes about building a sound track.

How They Do It

A major motion picture has a sound track made from hundreds of separate audio tracks. These are divided into four distinct categories. Dialogue needs no explanation, I hope. The others require some background to understand.

Music, Sound Effects, and Ambience

What is ambience? Ambience is the background noise in any particular location. If you are shooting at the airport, it is the sound of thundering jet engines. If you are shooting in the middle of a large auditorium, it is an empty echo sound. Sound effects include car doors opening and closing, gunshots, and any other sound that will enhance your film's impact. Finally, there's music. This is going to be your savior; nothing can make a scene come together better then the right piece of music. A few notes can instantly set the mood for a scene and help bring it to the emotional conclusion that most filmmakers strive for. In order to build up all of these sound tracks, a major feature film might employ upwards of twenty people. The studio will hire a composer to write an original score and then license the pop tunes that it wants. All of this adds up to big money. Once this crew is done assembling all these elements, they might have built up somewhere in the neighborhood of one hundred separate tracks. Now it's time to combine all these sounds in the right ratio to make the completed sound track. This is called the **sound mix.**

Forget About It

Now you must blank your mind of all the information above and everything else you have ever heard about sound from any soundperson-know-it-all from anywhere in the world. The major consideration in choosing your path to the ultimate sound track is going to be dictated by how you chose to edit the picture. Using the same technology for your sound work makes sense. You already have the equipment or know where to get it, and by this time you surely know how to work the machine. Utilize this equipment for the sound work, as well.

Film Sound Tracks

You have cut your film on a flatbed editing table. Your work print is a big sloppy mess of editing tape, grease pencil marks, and the occasional white leader slug that takes the place of three frames of film that you could not find. The whole mess is sticking together, and you are now ready to build your sound track. To build your sound track on a flatbed, you must have all your effects music and dialogue transferred to the sprocketed magnetic tape known as fullcoat. Fullcoat is the exact same size as 16-mm film, and the sprocket holes that run down one side are used to keep the audio in sync with the picture mechanically. Once you have transferred all your sound to fullcoat, you will cut each sound effect or music cue into a sound reel to correspond to the picture that you see on the flatbed editing screen. You will put a fill leader in between these sounds. (Remember that a fill leader is a single perforated film; in short, a print of somebody else's film—perhaps a person who didn't pay his lab bill.) You will cut the fill leader into your sound track so the base is facing toward the sound head. By doing so, you keep the sound heads clean of emulsion that would scrape off if you inserted the fill leader the other way around.

When you are done building all these reels of sound, you will bring them into a mixing facility where they will be threaded up on separate play machines and mixed down into your final sound track. Now, remember all those pieces of sound you taped into these reels? Yup, as you roll back and forth mixing your film, these tape splices stretch and bend and then finally break. Not only do splices break, but so do sprocket holes—and when they go, you lose sync. This is why this method of building a sound track and mixing your film sucks.

Building Linear Sound Tracks on a Video Editing System

You are going to make your movie with no more then six audio tracks, and it's going to sound great.

At this point, your whole movie has been edited together onto our video master. The only audio on the tape is the dialogue and the ambience that is behind the dialogue on track one. We are now going to strike two submasters onto another piece of video stock. Call these two submasters tape A and tape B. Beta SP is the best for this purpose because you can get used stock for cheap. It also comes in ninety-minute lengths, which is perfect for your eighty-four-minute movies. On each Beta SP tape, you will lay the dialogue onto the two AFM tracks (called tracks three and four). That leaves tracks one and two on each tape free. On tape A, you will use track one for music and track two for sound effects (SFX). On tape B, track one will also contain SFX and track two will be for what I call the cover SFX track. You will edit in sound effects and music utilizing the **insert edit mode** on your video controller. Insert editing allows you to edit one audio track while not affecting either the picture or the other audio tracks.

Once you have built up all these separate tapes containing your raw audio, you will bring them to a mix facility, where the technicians can use multiple video decks for playback. This way, all your videotapes can be played back at once. The technician can then adjust each tape's audio level and then rerecord them onto a master tape. Another alternative would be to dub each tape into a nonlinear audio system such as a Sonic Solutions or Pro Tools system. From there, the technician can mix your film's audio on a computer and then lay back the final mix onto your master videotape.

Building Non-linear Audio Tracks

Now that you know how sound tracks were built in the Dark Ages, let's move to the present. Today, all you need to know is one name: Pro Tools. This software runs on a Macintosh and is sold by a company named Digidesign, which is owned by Avid. Basically, what

Pro Tools gives you is the ability to build an almost unlimited number of audio tracks and then mix them together. Alternatively, you can output eight unmixed audio tracks from Pro Tools to a machine called a DA-88. You can then take all your DA-88 tapes to a professional sound studio and have it complete the mix for you.

Regardless of what nonlinear editing system you cut your film on, its audio features can be used to build and ultimately mix your film's sound track. Most nonlinear systems allow you to have at least eight tracks of audio; additionally, they all have a method of premixing these eight tracks down to two. This basically gives you the ability to build an unlimited number of audio tracks.

Spotting

The first step in building any sound track is **spotting,** the process by which you go through your film and make a list of all the sounds you will need to complete your sound tracks. Once you have compiled this list, you must get the sounds you need. First up, music.

Music

For this track, you will require the aid of a musician. But if you believe you have a smidgen of musical talent, you might want to score the movie yourself. Think about a John Carpenter movie. Remember the sound track? Well, not only is John a busy director, but by God he's stepping up to the plate and scoring his movies as well. So let John be your inspiration. Go watch *Escape from New York,* then dust off the old Casio and give it a whirl. I would recommend preset number 6. You are actually going to need two tracks for your music because you want this thing to be in stereo. Music tracks also include those low, rumbly things and other subtle mood-enhancing sounds that we all love.

A Musician Can Be a Dangerous Thing

It's a good thing that in this world we live in, everybody knows somebody who wants to become a rock 'n' roll, jazz, music-mixing superstar. It's an equally good thing that everybody who fits into that category is also dying to score a movie. Once you find such a person, offer a trade. He or she will get a large title in your movie and be reimbursed for the tape stock that is used. In exchange, you will get all the rights to the music he or she creates for your film.

Remember, these guys are living the rock 'n' roll fantasy. They are out late drinking hard and inhaling gases from prepackaged whipped cream canisters. These guys are killing off brain cells faster than you can say Jonestown. Are you going to let someone like that go off on his own and score your movie? *No Way*. He needs guidance. He needs to know what you want, and where in the movie you want it.

Give your musician a copy of your film with the temp music track you have assembled. From here, you can steer your musician in two directions. Direction number one asks him to blatantly rip off the music you have given him. It's truly amazing how a few well-placed notes can change a piece of well-known music into a totally original piece. Your musician may complain that you are stifling his creative energy. This leads you to your second option. Tell him to use the music as a guide, but that you would like him to create his own sound track for the film. Hold your ground. At least this way you will have some idea as to what you are getting. If you let him loose on his own, he may return with Benny Hill music that he insists would be perfect for the tender love scene.

Big Sound
Effects Track

What is a big sound effect? Gunshots are big. A man being crushed by a bus is also big. The world exploding into a nuclear fireball is big. Silk brushing against flesh is not big. Anything that will have a strong dramatic impact or that will be sorely missed if it is not in the movie will be considered a big sound and will be placed into this track.

So Where Am I Going to Find These Sounds?

Large record stores often carry sound effects CDs. Try and get the ones that are from the last fifteen years. The earlier ones are usually records that have been transferred to CD. Some of these may grace you with static, skips, and all the other hoopla that is inherent to vinyl.

If you can't find these CDs, don't despair. There is an easy way to record sound effects. It is with your friend's, mother's, or uncle's camcorder. And don't say you can't get one. Think back to that last family gathering. That's right, it's all coming back to you now. That fat guy in the stupid pants with the plaid pattern on a sea of puke green. That's right, the guy who was roaming around with that video camera. Of course, your first reaction will be denial; there is no way you could come from the same gene pool as that guy. But after a little while your need for the camera will win out. Contact your parents and have them contact Uncle Jimbo. They will tell you to call him yourself. So call him up and ask him if you can borrow his pride and joy, the camcorder that he got for a steal at the local electronic emporium because he knows what he is doing. The one that he paid over a $1,000 for ten years ago. The one that you saw advertised in

Sunday's paper for $200 at the place that has free balloons for the kids and has a going-out-of-business sale every third Wednesday.

Now that you are in possession of the camera, point it at the thing you need to record a sound from. Press the little red button and record the object producing sound. Being able to see the sound as well as hear it will help you later when it comes time to put the sounds into your movie. From here it's just a simple matter of hooking up the camcorder to your editing system of choice and rerecording the sounds into your sound track.

Ambience

Ambience is the natural background sound that occurs at any location. When a character talks, sure, you will hear his voice; but to a lesser extent you will also hear the Slurpee machine that he is standing next to. When you cut from a close-up to a wide shot, the soundman had no choice but to move his microphone farther away from the subject. The result is that the sound of the Slurpee machine is also fainter. You don't want the volume of this whirling crushed-ice-and-sugar-dispensing machine to jump up and down on every cut—that would be annoying, and it would probably make us hate frozen drinks forever. So you are going to build a sound track that only contains the sound of this machine and any other ambient sound in the room.

Remember that thirty seconds of silence on the set in Chapter 7? Well, this is when it counts, so let's hope you didn't elbow the DP and start cracking up. You will loop the ambient sound so you have enough to run continuously for the entire scene. When you are approaching a cut in your mix, you can gradually increase the level of the ambience track so it will cover the machine jump-in sound when you cut to the close-up, or vice versa.

Ambience for Effect

This is one of the best tracks for covering up flaws in your dialogue track. This track will consist of long, interesting environmental sounds for each location. It might be a babbling brook for the exteriors, or factory noises for the science lab. Just use some semblance of logic when selecting these sounds. Think about long, low rumbles or electricity arcing. Better yet, go rent *Eraserhead* and give it a listen.

Footsteps and Foley

Nobody notices footsteps, or do they? If you have a very quiet scene in which your character walks through a dance hall littered with peanut shells, you might just want to hear the sound of nuts cracking underfoot as your character heads toward his destiny. The act of borrowing your girlfriend's boots and walking in place to mimic the footsteps of your character and, most important, recording the sounds those boots make is known as **foley**. If you hire somebody to do this job for you, he or she is known as a foley artist.

ADVANCED SOUND THEORY NUMBER 1: **The more garbage you throw in, the less they notice.**

Say you have some dialogue that is very difficult to hear. The first thing you would think is this: I should try to clean this dialogue up and make it audible to humans as well as canines. But that's going to cost money. A better idea is to throw a lot of garbage sounds onto your other tracks. Fill them all up with loud background sound effects—for example, a buzz saw. For some reason, when you play back your dialogue with all these garbage sounds mixed in behind it, your characters will become more audible. The human mind will sort through all the garbage, dismiss it, and key in on the dialogue. Isn't the mind a wonderful thing?

Missing Dialogue: The Art of Fudging It

Nothing can be more traumatic than missing dialogue. Don't worry about it. There is something in the film industry known as **Automatic Dialogue Replacement (ADR).** In most industries across America, *automatic* means that something happens by itself with a minimum of labor. In the film business, *automatic* means what follows.

To replace the missing dialogue, you will bring your actor into a sound recording studio. There, in a soundproof room with headphones on, he or she will listen to a technician play back the line preceding the one that needs to be replaced. Simultaneously, a light will blink once, twice, and then three times. The third blink will be the actor's cue to begin speaking into the microphone to rerecord the line. The actor has to duplicate the inflection used when the line was originally recorded so that it matches up to the filmed lip movements.

Your job here is to keep it all together while trying to keep the costs and calories down. If you want to sound like you know what you're doing, you can say things to the actor like "Purse your lips," or "Lick your bottom lip, then say the line." Eventually, after many tries, you will be able to reassemble the missing dialogue. That sounds automatic, doesn't it?

In some rare instances, you might have done something to cause your actors to sever their ties with you. If you have no chance of getting the actors back for some ADR, just do your best impersonation and drop the dialogue in. Nobody will notice. Well, your actors might, but you're already done with them. So who cares?

ADR at Home

Make a VHS tape of the section of your film with the dialogue that must be replaced. Invite the actor over to check out your new Nintendo system and then ask if he would mind rerecording some lines of dialogue for you.

Place the microphone in front of the actor and get a good audio level. You can record into almost anything—and don't worry about timecode, because you are going to manually place these pieces of dialogue into your film's sound track. Press PLAY on the VCR and let the actor watch the piece to be recorded. The next time you hit PLAY, keep your hand on the TV's volume button; about three seconds before you reach the section of dialogue you want to replace, quickly lower the volume. In an ideal world, your actor will speak the lines at the right pace with the proper inflection. Work your way through the movie, replacing all the bad lines. Thank the actor for his or her time and you are done. Then just plug the new dialogue into your sound track. Don't forget to lay down a separate track of the ambient sound from the location (your house) so these new lines will weave seamlessly into your sound track.

This same setup can be used for home foley work. First spot the scene. This means that you watch it a couple of times and make a list of all the sounds you will need to create. The list might include leather rustling, leading to a knock on a door and a body thumping down, followed by a door slamming and then feet running down steps.

The Mix

This is truly an exciting time. You are going to see your movie with all the dialogue, music, and sound effects together for the first time. Sit back and enjoy it. As you mix your film, you will be adjusting all the sound levels. You will also want all the dialogue to be audible. *What did you say?* Again, I *said* to make sure all the dialogue is audible. Sometimes you may be tempted to swell the music in an effort to heighten the emotional impact of a scene, but don't drown out crucial dialogue. If you are mixing your film at home on your computer-based system, you can carefully go through each scene and adjust the volume of each audio track until you get them in the right proportion to each other. The important thing is to establish a base level. To do this, choose a level on the vu meter that is high enough to give you a good solid recording, but not so high as to peek out and distort the sound if someone yells a line. You will also want to set the level of your amplifier to be consistent throughout the mix. Once you move the volume to your preferred level, take a grease pencil and make a mark next to the knob or slider.

Going Back to Your Master, the M and E Tracks

When you sell your film to a foreign market, it will be dubbed into another language. In order for the buyers to change the language of your film, they are going to need a sound track of the master that contains no dialogue. This is known as the M and E (music and effects) sound tracks. Sometimes it's easier to make these at the same time your are mixing your film; sometimes it's not. Just keep the M and E track in mind because you don't want to throw anything away that you might need. Foreign markets are huge and worth preparing your film for. But if you sell your film, don't take payment in Euros.

Film festivals

Once you have completed your film, you will quickly realize that your work has just begun. The next step is getting your film distributed. How does one do that, you ask? Today the name of the game is film festivals, and they are sprouting up faster than you can say $40 entry fee. The good news is that there are so many festivals, you should be able to get your film into at least one.

The bad news, like everything else in this country, is that most film festivals are designed to make money. Like all businesses, some are very good at taking care of their customer's needs and some are very bad, but both types seem to be very good at taking care of their customer's money. Festival entrance fees range anywhere from $25 to $500. You could easily spend thousands in these fees alone, so you have to be careful to maximize your investments.

The first step is to develop an overall festival plan. Keep in mind that once you get into one festival, it is much easier to get into the next. OK, here's step one: You are going to target a festival you think your completed film might have a good chance of getting accepted by. There are a couple of places to start. First, investigate any local film festivals. Most of the smaller local festivals will be more inclined to accept a film from a hometown filmmaker. The benefits to this kind of festival are increased press coverage and the ability to demonstrate that it is indeed giving back to the community and the businesses that it hits up to pay for the festival expenses. These are angles you may want to touch upon as you pester the festival directors with inquiries about the status of your film.

Strategy for Getting Your Film Screened at a Local Festival

If you have the foresight, you could volunteer to work at your local film festival this year, knowing that you will be submitting your feature film next year. As you work the festival, make no mention of your filmmaking aspirations. Do endear yourself to the festival directors and screening committee. To do this you will utilize your personality as well as the fact you were the first guy to buy a round of beers at the local pub. Once you have laid this necessary groundwork, it should be a cinch to get your new friends to program your film into their next festival.

If you are not interested in volunteer work, there are other ways to get into a festival. Sure, you could just go out and make a good film; but if you think that guarantees your film's being accepted, you have a lot to learn about the way things work. That brings us to the number one rule of how things work: "Who do you know?" Perhaps a friend is a sponsor of the festival? If he can put in a good word for you and your film you might just get some kind of preferential treatment. Now let's be perfectly clear here: you have no interest in being another videotape in a pile of manila envelopes. I cannot stress enough how you must utilize all the weapons at your disposal to further you and your film career. Let the other guy cling to his idea that if it's meant to happen, it will happen. Let him watch his dreams fade as he works the fryalator at the local fast-food restaurant. Well, now he is stuck. If he doesn't get promoted to short-order cook, he's not going to be able to pay his bills. As all this is going on, he is waiting for a response from the film festival he entered with a film that was probably much better than yours; but that letter never comes, and neither does the promotion and now he's not only working the fryalator but also a security job at the local CVS. Don't let this happen to you. No, you are about action and making it happen. If you ever are in doubt about making or not making a call, then make the damn call.

The Rest of the Fests

Like movies, film festivals fall into categories or genres. Some festivals specialize in horror or shocking films: they are usually called the (name of city held) Underground Film Festival. Another category is the religious or ethnic film festival. If you are a Zulu filmmaker, it stands to reason that you will have a better-than-average chance of getting into the Zulu Filmmaker Summer Festival held each year in the Catskill Mountains. So take a minute and figure out what kind of film you have made—and for that matter, see where you came from and then search the various festival guides or the Internet for the festivals that match up to your strengths. Those that match up will become your first round of targets.

The next step letting yourself be known. Nobody ever got thrown out of the film business for sticking out, and that's exactly what you need to do if you are going to get into the festival of your choice. Today, the average festival gets thousands of submissions and might accept fifty from that number. If you're playing the odds, you might have better luck at the roulette wheel—at least you have a 50 percent chance with that. (Yes, I know technically it's not 50 percent because of the two green spaces, but this book is about filmmaking, not roulette.) Now some of you might say that you don't need to do this because your film is good, or great, or the best thing since spray-on hair and that you will let it be judged on its merits. Well, this would be a great argument if we lived in some Marxist society where film festivals actually judged film that way. Unfortunately for you, there are a number of criteria that festivals use in accepting films: the day of the week; the position of the moon; and what your film can do for the festival so it can look like a great big important event and get a really big vodka company to sponsor one of the parties next year. That's where the festivals are coming from.

My Film Got Accepted to a Film Festival; Now What?

If you have chosen to make an independent film, the first step in your distribution plan is film festivals. That's right, I said distribution plan. Even though you might like to believe that you are entering festivals to garner awards, the main goal is actually to get your film seen by an audience. Within that audience there will hopefully be a film critic or two, and perhaps a representative from another festival. The representative from the other festival will be so impressed by your audience response that she will have no choice but to invite your film to participate in that festival. You will then use these items to make up a press kit. Now it's on to the second round of festivals. We will call these the Springboard Alpha Delta Romeo Film Festival, or SADRAFF for short. Why this crazy name? Well, we are going to treat this whole process like a military mission; after all, you are out to conquer the film world.

The SADRAFF festivals include many festivals you have heard of, such as the Sundance, New Director New Films, Telluride, and South by Southwest film festivals. The result you hope to garner from this second group of festivals is a distribution deal with a reputable distributor. *Reputable* means a distributor who will return your phone calls. A distributor who will tell you how your film is doing and sit down with you and formulate a plan about how to maximize the profit potential for your film. Ultimately, *reputable* means the distributor will give you a fair share of the film proceeds when it comes time to divvy up the money. If your distributor is in bankruptcy court like mine, let's call it X Cinema, and you had to find out about it because one day you noticed its Internet site was no longer up and running, then I would say this is a surefire sign that your distributor may not be reputable.

What to Do at a Film Festival

OK, you made it. Your flight has touched down and you, the crew, and several tag-along actors and some guy who just loves to party but nobody is really sure where he has come from have piled into a hotel room. And now the first challenge has come up—securing a place to sleep. Sure you could fight it out for the bed, and maybe you could even get it for yourself—but it's not going to be very comfortable. And you will have little to no privacy because that's where everybody is going to hang out and watch TV all night.

Get yourself a backpack and a foam bed pad made for camping. You can now carve out your own little piece of real estate. The first place to look is the closet; if it's big enough, well, you just got yourself a private room for one.

Flyering (Is That a Word?)

Just because your film has been chosen to play at a film festival does not mean that anybody will show up to watch it. The film festival people are going to do what they can for your film, but beyond sending out a few copies and giving you a good date for your screening there is little more they can do for you.

So now the ball is in your court, and the first order of business is to get bodies into seats. Sure you would like to get reviewers and distributors to attend, but a screening without bodies is a failure.

The first step, short of busing people in, a trick that some films with deep pockets can afford to do, is publicity. Get the title of your film out to the average person in the city you are playing. You need twenty-four-inch-by-thirty-inch posters that have the name of your film, some kind of captivating imagery, and the screening time and location.

Arm yourself with a staple gun, some clear packing tape, and some good running shoes, and hit the streets. You want to target any location where film people are likely to congregate, then start putting up your posters. Don't put them on storefronts. (The owners will rip them down.) Don't put them on telephone poles. (In most cities this is illegal.) Do put them on those wooden walls around construction sights, as well as those newspaper dispensers for the local rag.

Here is another tip. When the police arrive—run. If you decide to wait around and see what they want, they might arrest you. This happened to me in New York City and I did not go to jail. Why? Because of the title of this book. If I had gone to jail, I would have had to change it, wouldn't I.

The IFFM—Then and Now

The Independent Feature Film Market (IFFM) is held in New York City at the Angelika Film Center every September. For ten days this market takes over all the screens in this underground theater complex. They show everything from works in progress to completed theatrical films with distribution deals in place.

Several years ago I took a work in progress to the IFFM. It was titled *Road to Park City*. Before we could celebrate, we found out when our film was scheduled to screen. We were assigned the worst screening slot that can be imagined. *Road To Park City* would be shown on a Sunday—the last day of a ten-day movie market. To be exact, we were the last film screened on the last day of the market. We sucked it up and proceeded to plaster flyers all around the theater for the seven days before our screening. When we arrived at the theater on Sunday morning, we noticed a severe drop-off in attendance. It seems that most of the film buyers were getting over their hangovers from the Sundance party the night before, or else they were packing up to get out of town.

Finally, 6:30 P.M. arrived and the door to our theater opened. Much to our shock, we were a sellout; not one seat was left in the theater. In fact, people were sitting in the aisle, and some were holding the door open in the back of the theater as others tried to get a glimpse of our film. In short, a great screening. Afterward, a guy from HBO and several other representatives approached us about our film. Some lunatic who said he was the founder of the U.S. film festival that became the Sundance Film Festival demanded that we give him our poster. We left that screening walking on a cloud. Now, I don't know what to attribute that great turnout to, but one thing is for sure: We did a great job of covering the area with our posters. We also had our lead actor stand outside the theater all day and bark at anybody who crossed his path.

The next year we finished our film, and again we thought it might be a good idea to go back to the IFFM. So we packed up our film along with our credit card information and waited to get assigned our screening slot, hoping to improve on the position we held the year before. With a finished film we felt we could capitalize on any inquiries from potential distributors.

Well, we didn't get in. That's right, the IFFM didn't accept us. It felt our film was not right for its market. The IFFM is entitled to this position, of course, but it did strike us as kind of odd. One year we were acceptable, and it gladly charged our AMEX card the $500 fee to attend; the next year we were not, but the sponsors still made us join the Independent Feature Project (IFP) even though we didn't get in. To add insult to injury, I didn't even get the subscription to *Filmmaker* magazine that comes along with this forced membership due to some kind of data entry problem. Am I bitter? No. Will I submit a future project? Well, let's just say that I reserve the right to change my mind at any moment. Is this typical of the film business? I would say yes.

The Lay of the Land

Once you arrive at the film festival du jour you have to get the lay of the land quickly in order to operate as efficiently as possible. First you are going to need to know the locations of all the hospitality tents and any other rooms set up for filmmakers that contain food. These are usually in a conference room of the hotel that the festival has conned into sponsoring the festival that year. You'll know you have arrived by the abundance of celery sticks and Diet Cokes. This is it, your very own restaurant. Once you are inside, make friendly with the hotel workers whose job it is to resupply the room with miniature foods and shaved vegetables. Perhaps you have an allergy to everything they have put out? Then it would be perfectly within your rights to request something more to your liking. More often than not, the staff will be happy to comply. Tip the waiter or waitress a five spot and you can almost guarantee a continual supply of food.

Next up? The festival's mail system. Usually, this is comprised of a bunch of wooden boxes with a number below them. This is how the festival will communicate with you. It is also how you can attempt to communicate with distributors and other people of importance. The only drawback is that every other filmmaker will be trying to communicate in a similar manner, so it's not going to be your best avenue for success.

Next, and possibly most important, is the bar that the festival staff will be hanging out in. Your best chance of getting in is to try and cozy up with the festival director and all of his or her minions, and nothing lubricates these relationships more than some good old alcohol. Once they are comfortable with you, they might take pity on you and steer you toward the distributor who is enjoying a martini across the bar or the newspaper critic drinking the Sambuca by the video bowling machine.

Party Until You Drop

Sometimes the most important part of a film festival is the parties that go on around it. You should plan on sleeping through a few films during the middle of the day so you have the maximum amount of energy to party through the night. There is nothing like a documentary on the grazing habits of elk to give you a much-needed break in the middle of the day. After the elk film, you will be refreshed and ready to mingle. The goal here is to meet people, and not just any people. You should be on the lookout for those who could possibly further your film's chance of getting distribution. The trick is not to appear as if you care about films or filmmaking. If you meet a distributor at a party and launch into a tirade about your film, you will probably scare away this possible future contact. The rule here is simple: whenever you meet anybody for the first time, you are not allowed to talk about your film. Instead, talk about the grazing habits of the wild North American elk.

I'll Go to Your Film If You Go to Mine

What you are really saying is this: "I need to check out your film so I can be confident that mine is better so I'll get more attention and win some kind of prize at this festival, but in the meantime I'll pretend to be your friend and use you because you have a rental car and I don't." This attitude is often the result of your film being in some kind of competition at a festival. How can you be expected to make friends with those you wish to beat in competition? To tell you the truth, you would be better off palling around with filmmakers who are involved in another competition that you can feign an interest in.

The Art of
Sneaking into
Parties

The secret is to prearrange. For this you need to switch to your alter ego: an employee at a PR firm. We are going to set up two identities for you. The first is you as yourself, a struggling filmmaker with a gung ho attitude and the unflappable ability to cover a ten-foot-square section of wall with flyers in less than five seconds. The second is the obnoxious PR person. The PR you is going to take care of all the arrangements for the filmmaker you. The best way to get into parties is to mention you are a PR person who is handling a bunch of other films. You can then call the PR people who are representing the films and parties you wish to get into. They will want to come to your parties and, of course, you will want to go to theirs. After you have secured their passes, it's a simple matter to cancel your parties.

A few other key items to carry around with you are a rainbow assortment of Magic Markers. These are often needed to mimic the mark placed on your hand in order to regain access to a party.

Also keep in mind that two passes can often get ten to twenty people into a party. The process is called the walkout. One guy walks out with two passes, then two people walk into the party. Repeat step one until all members of your posse are inside the party.

My Film Rules

This is the attitude you are going to need if you want to be successful. How many times have you gotten excited about somebody else's film after they have said this to you: "Well, it's pretty good, but we ran out of light and the cat ran off in the middle of the scene, but I think it kind of tells the story if I can give you the backstory before the film starts."

We all like to be honest, but in this industry you have to be able to suppress this trait. If anybody asks you about your film, spew forth only enthusiasm and excitement when you talk. Before attending any screening, meeting, or other business related to your film, you must do the following exercise.

Look in a mirror and repeat the following phrase three times, each time yelling a little louder: My film rules! MY film rules! MY FILM RULES! OK, now go out there and talk up a storm about the greatest piece of cinema since *Castro Street*.

Have Your Own Party

After much debate, we decided that we should have our own party during Slamdance. After carefully examining our options, it was somehow decided that a breakfast party after the 9 A.M. screening on Wednesday would be the best move. Actually, it was a very bad move on our part.

If you are going to have a party, make sure it's at night, with tons of booze and a crazy name like the ZOOMA, ZOOMA, ZOOMA Party. Try to build some kind of mystique around your party. Spread rumors about how insane it was last year, even though it didn't happen last year. Go to town, and you might just have a killer party.

Hiring a PR Firm

You might as well cover yourself with dollar bills and walk through Central Park at night because the same result is very likely. You're going to get mugged. I hope this doesn't sound too negative, but unless a PR firm has something tangible that it can use to help you promote your film, it is probably not going to do you one ounce of good.

Lawyers

You are going to need them. A lawyer might even help you sell your film, so I would suggest finding one before you need one. Unfortunately, the guy who represented you at the closing of your house will not be adequate to represent you and your film when it comes time to negotiate a deal. There are many lawyers who advertise in the various magazines that cater to the independent filmmakers. I would say this would be as good a place as any to begin your search.

The 9 A.M. Screening Spot

Slit your wrists and go home. That would be too easy, wouldn't it? No, this is going to be a character-building experience. When you get through this, you are going to be a better man or woman, and maybe a tad more bitter about the whole process. Here is a tip: If you arrive at the theater and it is being vacuumed, you are in trouble. Tough it out. Put on a good face and go to your film's screening.

I Got a Bad Feeling About This

OK, your film has been accepted to the Gold Coast Film Festival, and you are really excited to go see your film projected to the myriad film buffs who must surely flock to this great festival every year. So you book the airline tickets and drag three of your friends along with you. Upon getting to your hotel, you decide to take a walk down to the theater that the festival has rented for the week to show its selected films. That's when it hits you.

With each step through the deserted streets of this once thriving beach community, your stomach gets tighter and tighter. When you finally reach the theater, you don't know what to do first—puke or take a dump. Because now you know that this was a huge waste of time. Nobody is going to pay homage to your film at this Mecca. But being an optimist, you decide to ask the salesperson how many tickets have been sold to your show. And that is when the gruesome reality truly sets in. Yes, you have flown all the way to the Gold Coast so you can sit in an auditorium with three senior citizens. Lesson learned? You don't have to go to every festival your film gets accepted into. Sometimes you should save the money and send the print instead, then ask the festival people to send any newspaper articles or reviews written about your film.

The Road To Park City (What Happened at Slamdance with Our Film); Or Beware of the ChapStick

It was day eight in Park City. The next day they would announce the festival winners, and we had not heard a peep. The tension in our group was running a little hot, so we decided to go out for some hamburgers—the thought being that some red meat would make us feel better. I looked over to the next table and there was one of the cofounders of the film festival sharing a table with someone. Well, I gave him the standard subdued nod signifying that yes, I had seen him but no, I wasn't going to walk over to his table and make a big scene in front of his guest.

After my gesture, I got back to the real business at hand—the quest for red meat. No sooner had I decided on the Park City burger with cheese than I heard a voice saying, "Here, Bret, looks like you could use this." Thrust before me was a tube of ChapStick. And then I knew. We would win nothing at the festival. I meekly reached a hand out and took the tube of ChapStick, thanked the festival cofounder, and decided that yes, I wouldn't win, but at least my lips would be both moisturized and protected from the sun. This was surely better than being given the audience award, thereby gaining an extra screening of my film that would be attended by many industry folks and dramatically increase the chance of its acquiring some type of distribution.

That night after the awards were announced, we went to the

American Steak House to be exact, a place where they claim to heat your plate up to 500 degrees. Why? I have no idea, but the idea is intriguing all the same.

As I sat there with my silky smooth lips and kiln-fired plate, I had another reaction. Should I have accepted the ChapStick in the first place? What is the proper social response when one is offered ChapStick by a festival director?

The point is this. If your film is going to win any award at a festival, you are going to know about it in advance. It may be as simple as the festival director asking you your travel plans or recommending that you attend a certain event. Like the ChapStick, these are clues about your film's standing with the festival folks.

The Web of Lies

As you progress along your filmmaking odyssey, you will leave behind a trail of half-truths, fibs, exaggerations, and outright lies. In the beginning, this will be of no consequence, but as you move deeper and pile story upon story on anybody willing to listen, the rules of the game will change. You have to keep your stories straight because someday, somewhere, when you are racing to get a shot off because the sun is setting, a security guard is going to walk over and ask why you are filming a scene at a national park when all you applied for was a fishing license. While I condone creative speech, do keep it in check.

chapter 13

You have **enough** going against you, so let's go on to chapter **14**

Marketing and distribution

t he film is done. You are a lot thinner and beginning to take on the shape of one of those elbow noodles from the macaroni-and-cheese dinners that have become your main food staple over the last few months. Well, congratulations! You are now two-thirds of the way there. Sure you have been to a bunch of festivals, and your film by your accounts was far above the competition. But as you sit around waiting to jet off to the next festival, you begin to realize that you have not made one cent from this cinematic exercise. Furthermore, in order to make your next film, you are going to need to make a profit from the first one. So where do you go to get the money? For this, you do not have many options.

You can stick your film under your arm and hightail it out to Hollywood, confident that you have a secure future in feature-film production. The idea here would be to shop your film around to the many distributors that call this city, which looks like a suburb, their home. But this can just as easily be accomplished through the mail. Before you do anything, you should have a general idea of what markets you are trying to sell your film to.

Remember that right now your feature exists on Digital Betacam or a similar high-quality video format. You cannot project videotape, nor can you hold it up to the light and look at the little pictures on it. So you have two basic markets open to you at this point: home video and television (which includes cable television, pay-per-view television, satellite television . . . gee, there is a lot of television out there) and, of course, the Internet.

The Internet and Your Film

By this time, everybody is familiar with *The Blair Witch Project,* and anybody who follows the stock market is also aware of the dot-com meltdown. So what can be learned from these two things other than the fact that your kids no longer have enough money to go through four years of college, and that you are not going to be able to retire at age thirty-five?

First, I think we can safely say that you are not going to buy your pet food on the Web (or, for that matter, gift certificates, groceries, vitamins, or beauty products). But what you will buy is a Web site, and at this Web address you will create a place where everybody in the world can go to find out information about your movie. Remember Ben Kingsley in the movie *Sneakers?* He said that the most important thing in the world is information, and that the person who controls the information will control the world. Well, let's face it, we all hope we can learn something from the movies, even though our heart is telling us we are just being subjected to mindless entertainment so a huge international corporation can raise its share price and use this newfound clout to pad the pocket of important politicians and thereby influence the world to be more friendly to global expansion. But I would rather believe in Ben. And even though he was a misguided master criminal, perhaps I can learn from his mistakes.

The information. Right now, you know a whole lot about your film. It can only benefit you to have a place where anybody in the world can go and instantly find out every little detail about your movie project, and that place is called your movie's very own Web page.

Your Web Page

The Web page is easier then you think to get up and running. Chances are whoever is your Internet provider has the ability to host a Web site. Your first stop is finding a domain name. Log onto Network Solutions or one of the other domain name services and type away. Find the best name you can and then register it.

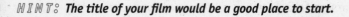 *HINT:* **The title of your film would be a good place to start.**

You should have a couple of crucial pieces of information on your Web site. First, you want to have any press you have garnered to this point available for viewing. You should have a quick, one-paragraph description of your film, and you should plan on having your trailer available for download so any interested parties can see a clip from your film. Finally, the most important thing is a person that interested parties can contact if they have any more questions about the film. That is all you need.

I wouldn't waste time trying to come up with complicated animated opening sequences that take time to load. I don't know about you, but I tend to get really turned off by slow-loading Web pages with an animation sequence that may or may not work on my browser. Just lay out the crucial information in an easy-to-understand format and move on to the next aspect of your never-ending quest to get your film into the right hands.

Distributors

If your film makes a big splash at a festival, or if you garner some good reviews in one of the trades, you might find yourself fielding phone calls from a film distribution company. Now you have to ask yourself: Why would a company call me and inquire about my film? No, it's not because they are patrons of the arts, nor is it because they see a glimmer of talent and want to be around for your next picture.

There is only one reason for this phone call, and that's *money*. Distributors are in business to make money, and if they believe your film has some kind of monetary potential that they can exploit you for, you can be sure that they will go after it.

Now look at the other side of the coin. You have sent your film out to thirty or so distributors. After a couple of weeks have passed, you have not received a phone call. How can this be? Surely your film should be picked up by one of these companies and distributed to the paying masses. The reality is that thirty companies have not called you back, and it might be time to come to grips with the fact that the economic impact of your film may be severely handicapped. At this point, you may have no other alternative than to self-distribute your film. But you persist: "Maybe my film got lost in the shuffle somewhere and perhaps a few phone calls could get it into the proper hands." If only you could get a personal meeting with the distributor, surely you could sway him to pick up your film.

This brings us to the meeting. You are now sitting outside the office of a person you know nothing about, but you are willing to put your film into his hands because he has an office. After all, what could be more legitimate than a person with an office?

What Happens When Your Tape Arrives at the Film Distributor

They carefully inspect the packaging, because if they didn't give you some secret little code to write on the outside of the package, they are going to immediately toss it into the garbage. No, they won't . . . I hope. If you have the code, your film will move up to the top of the pile next to all the other tapes that have the code. This pile, of course sits above the pile of tapes that have just been randomly sent in with some kind of letter of introduction.

The next thing that happens is the higher-ups at the company will give their Ivy League intern a pile of films to look at over the weekend. Now, this intern has decided to go rock climbing with his significant other. So, on Sunday night when he returns from that dream weekend of rock climbing, he will set aside some time to view these tapes. Knowing all that, what do you think the chances are of this intern recommending your film for possible acquisition and distribution after being screened at eight times regular speed? Not a very pretty picture, is it?

The second and third tiers are not as layered, so you may have varying degrees of success with them. The smaller the company, the easier it will be to crack the bosses' defense system and get the right person on the phone. From there, it is up to you to sell your film. But the lower on the tier the company is, the harder it will be to collect any royalties due to you. There are surely some exceptions to this rule, but I have yet to encounter one.

So why are you going through all these traumas and great pains to get your film in the hands of a distributor and never make a profit? The answer is simple: You want people to see your work, which is why you are willing to put a little faith in mankind, holding onto the hope that you have put your film in good hands.

Home Video

That's right, your film should be in that New Release section of your local video store any day now. There are several ways your film can be sold in the video market. And if you play your cards right, you may have a chance to have your film in the Mecca of home video—Blockbuster.

Video distribution, like every other aspect of filmmaking, is based on whom you know and what they can do for you. If you don't know any buyers for the major video store chains across the USA, you might want to consider teaming up with a video distribution company that does. Video distribution companies specialize in packaging, promoting, and selling your videotape to get it into the proper distribution channels.

Foreign

Your distributor will also be selling the theatrical, home video, and television rights to your film to all the nations in the world. The rights will be sold for a straight fee per territory. You will get the most money from countries like Japan and Germany, and the least from Poland and Tibet. The good thing here is that there are many countries craving American entertainment. The bad news is this is an almost impossible task for an independent filmmaker to pull off. You will almost certainly be forced to trust your film to a distributor to handle this segment of the film market.

Film Markets

Every year there are three major film markets and many more smaller ones. They are the American Film Market in Los Angeles, which is usually held in late February to early March; Cannes in the south of France, which takes place around May; and Miffed in Milan, Italy, which takes place around August.

Film distributors travel to these film markets to sell their films. Buyers from around the world come to the markets to buy films. These markets usually last a week or more, and a distributor will see hundreds of buyers from many countries. The name of the game is hype your product. The distributor who has the prettiest girl in the smallest outfits, along with the sexiest posters, will usually fare much better then the older Jewish men who are offering hard sucking candies and quoting ancient proverbs to all those who approach. Sounds easy, you say. I'll just take my girlfriend to Victoria's Secret, buy a plane ticket online, and, with my film tucked under my arm, go to a film market. Well, that would be nice—but the cost of entry is a little more.

The people who run these markets are also in business to make money. Are you noticing a trend here? And to make money, they will rent you an office in the film market where you can set up and sell your film. Just like McDonald's, they will also try to upsell you. Perhaps you would like a screening of your film. No problem, just fork over $1,000. Say you want to park in the hotel where you have bought a room that is now your office. No problem, a parking pass can go for as much as $500. You get the picture. All this for the hope of selling your film to a few foreign territories. Priceless.

Star Factor

There is nothing that makes a distributor's job easier than having the name of a huge star to throw around every time they talk about your film. That's right, a bona fide star. A name people recognize, because if they recognize it then the Dalai Lama will recognize it and buy the foreign rights to the movie in India.

Distributors are not looking for names like Jack Nicholson or Julia Roberts, although they would jump at the chance to pick up a film with one of these A-list stars. No, they are looking for Eric Estrada and George Kennedy and other actors who are recognizable but past their prime. Or they are looking for the first work of a star that has just entered the limelight. Perhaps the student film that Bruce Willis worked on when he was a struggling actor. Or they might go for controversy, meaning a film starring somebody involved in some type of scandal that has been a major news story. These are the Fawn Halls and the Jessica Hahns, or maybe a pornstar trying to cross over into semirespectable filmmaking.

Then we have what I like to call the **stretch marketing** campaign. The stretch reads something like this: *Bloodhounds*, starring Joey Williams from *Die Hard* and *Die Hard 2*. So what part did Joey play in the *Die Hard* series, you ask? Well, chances are he was an extra who walked through the background outside of Nakatomi Plaza in the first one or was actually in the airport when Bruce Willis pulls up outside in the second one. While this is deceptive, it is a wildly acceptable practice when distributors produce sales materials and video box covers for their product.

For the art film, stretch marketing involves film festivals. While everybody would like to claim they won the grand jury prize at Sundance, only a very few actually do. But perhaps you went to Sundance last year, and maybe you had a VCR and a television and a tape of your film. You could now say something to the effect that you had played at Sundance—or if your film was in a festival but didn't win anything, you could always claim it was special selection or some other thing that makes your film stand out from the pack. The other essential part of exploiting film festival screenings are the little oak-leaf half wreaths that always surround the award a film has won at a festival. But we know there is no reason these little clusters cannot surround other equally important-sounding information.

Can You Afford a Lawyer?

Through creative bookkeeping, it is very easy for distributors to keep every cent your movie makes for themselves. The key words or phrases to watch out for are "cost of business," "distribution fee," or "recoupment of monies." All these mean essentially the same thing: We keep all the money and you get nothing.

After spending what was left of your 401k on your film, you are faced with a more harrowing situation. Yes, you are going to spend money on a lawyer. We all know that these guys don't come cheap, so is it really worth spending potentially thousands of dollars to collect hundreds of dollars in video sale royalties? This is something you will have to weigh out on a case-by-case basis.

Four-Walling It

Did you know that you can rent a theater and book your film into it, and then keep all the ticket sales for yourself? It's done every day, and this is a viable distribution alternative. A couple of things to keep in mind: Getting your film into the theater is only half the

 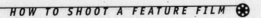

battle. The more important battle is getting warm bodies into the seats, and to do this you are going to need a marketing campaign and a boatload of friends.

There are a few independent-friendly cinemas. Two that come to mind are Lemelles in Los Angeles and Two Boots Pioneer Theater in New York. Both of these theaters will be glad to take a look at your film for a possible theatrical booking. Lemelles has midnight screenings at several of its theaters and will allow you to book your film into this spot on Friday and Saturday nights. If you can bring in enough people, the theater will keep the film playing indefinitely. Again, the key here is to fill the seats.

Self-Distribution

Let's forget about all these crooks and look into the possibility of distributing your own film. Is it possible? Sure. Will you succeed? Maybe. Will your bank lend you seed money? Not on your life. Self-distribution is a little bit akin to the good old American road trip. You are going to make one, possibly two, print(s) of your film. You are then going to call theaters throughout the country and speak to the managers. You will quickly win them over and convince them to book your film into their theater. If you want to see the country and drop out of society for a year or so, this is the route for you. If not, I don't recommend it.

Promotion

To be a hit in America, your film needs promotion. Be creative here. Plaster your own posters around town. Try and get it on your local cable program. Do anything you can to get the word out. The more creative you are, the more people will remember you—and the more successful your marketing campaign will be.

A big part of your marketing campaign is going to be something called **guerrilla marketing.** This means you take advantage of and exploit any and all opportunities to promote your film, even if they might be slightly illegal. The basics of guerrilla marketing involve placing stickers with your film's title all over town, perhaps covering equipment owned by your local telephone company or the newspaper boxes that sit at every corner, yelling out to be wrapped in color Xeroxes and packing tape.

The best place to get ideas is from the local bands in your area. Take a look around and see where they are placing flyers for their club dates. These would be as good a place as any for you to place a flyer about your film.

The Poster Box Cover

To properly promote your film, you are going to need a poster. This piece of artwork will also be used for making flyers that you will use at film festivals to promote your film, as well as postcards and ultimately the video box cover. You can see that you are going to get a lot of use out of this design so it is worth it to get it right. Your poster should look like a professional piece of artwork. It should include your film's name and the credits, as well as any other information that helps you convey what your film is about. The most important thing about your poster is its **curb appeal.** That means the poster has to make people stop in their tracks and study it, and then make them curious enough about your film to want to go see it.

The first decision is this: Are you going to design the poster yourself, or are you going to hire a professional graphic designer to handle this chore? First, go to the local video store. Walk up and down the aisle and see what box covers catch your eye. Rent four or five examples of box artwork that you would like to emulate, borrow, or blatantly steal the designs from. The next step is the local multiplex. Again, walk through the lobby and take a look at the posters. The purpose of this step is to make sure you see what the professionals are doing today; you are checking out the trends.

About ten years ago, the trend was to draw a rather large representation of the lead character in your movie somewhere on the poster. Today this is almost never done. The point is you don't want your artwork to look dated or out of step with the times—unless, of course, you are making a conscious decision to go retro, in which case this approach is OK. Either way, you are now going to utilize those production stills you took during the shooting of your film. By combining these stills with some catchy text, you should end up with your poster art. Another consideration should be sex. That's right, sex sells. We all know that, and why should your film poster be any different?

Trailer

The second most important promotional tool is the trailer. You are going to need a coming attraction for your movie. After editing your film, you should have a good idea of the best shots and some key words of dialogue that will help convey your story. You should plan on cutting a trailer that lasts no more then two minutes. Make sure your trailer is entertaining or funny, because the worst thing a trailer can be is boring. If you can't keep people entertained for two minutes, how can you be expected to do it for two hours—or in your case, eighty-four minutes?

They Went
Bankrupt, I Never
Saw a Cent, and
Now My Film Is
Floating Around in
Never-Never Land

So now that I have gotten you all pumped up to find a distributor, let me tell you a little story about a film called *Road to Park City*. Yes, it's my film.

The other day, I called my distributor to get a quarterly update on the sales of *Road to Park City*. The odd thing was that the number I dialed had been disconnected with no forwarding number. Well, that seemed to be a strange way to do business, but I reasoned I hadn't called the distributor in the previous six months, so maybe the forwarding option from the phone company had expired. I think this was the lie I told myself as I typed up an e-mail and sent it off to the president of a company we'll call X Cinema.

I received an e-mail in reply that went something like this: We have gone bankrupt. That is the reason you have received no communication from us in the last six months. If you want to get your film back, please contact the bankruptcy attorney who is in charge of our case.

This e-mail came to my attention just about a month after that distribution company had sold the home video and DVD rights to my film to another company we'll call Y Cinema. Y Cinema still had a phone, so I figured I would try to contact them in regard to the money they owed on VHS and DVD sales. I spoke to the owner of the company on the phone and inquired about where the royalty check would go if X Cinema were out of business. Well, he wasn't sure, but he was certain about one thing: It wouldn't be going to me, the filmmaker, the guy who financed the film with his own money, the guy who dragged all his friends into the nightmare of independent filmmaking. No, this was the one person he was absolutely sure would not be getting the money. What he said was this: "You should get yourself a lawyer."

So if I were to shamelessly promote my film *Road to Park City* in this book and suggest every reader go out and buy a copy, I would receive absolutely nothing from each and every sale generated. I'm getting a little depressed just thinking about this. I truly do like my film, and I think it has an interesting commentary about independent filmmaking. But why would I want to generate sales for a distribution company that doesn't even have the decency to let me know the status of my film?

Basically, beware. Just because you find a distributor, you may not be any better off because of it. Even if your film does make money, you still have to collect it.

Sue Me

Your final promotional tool is the lawsuit. Nothing generates press faster than a lawsuit. So try to get somebody to sue you over something really sensational. Or you can sue somebody claiming they stole your idea.

If you can't get a lawsuit, you might want to consider offending some special interest groups. When they show up with picket signs outside of the theater showing your film, you will have pulled off a publicity coup worth thousands of dollars. Think of *The Last Temptation of Christ* or *Dogma*. Both of these films generated massive amounts of publicity because a special interest group chose to target them. Hopefully, they will set their sights on you and your little film.

Other stuff you need to know

Name-Dropping

There is always one guy on every set who feels he is above the level of everybody else. He is the guy who picks all the cheese off a slice of pizza and throws away the crust. He is also the guy who tells story upon story about his run-in with Harrison Ford and how Sean Penn became his best buddy. In short, he is a name-dropper. Name-droppers are an interesting breed, but by reliving their glory days on your set they tend not to be the most useful crew members. And while they build up their own cult following of PAs and kraft service people, they drain precious resources from your set. So get all the name-dropping and storytelling out of the way right here and now.

Did I tell you about the time I was working for Steven Spielberg. Oh, yeah. He hired me to do a shoot for him, and I must say it was quite a joy.... You know what, I've never been very good at name-dropping. The shoot I did was for the Shoah Foundation. So while I did work for him in name, he never called me. In fact, my only contact was with a volunteer who told me where and when to show up, and about five hundred other cameramen from across the country also worked on this project. Name-dropping stories are oftentimes not as interesting as they may first sound.

The Meeting with a Hollywood Connection

It's unbelievable, but one of those phone numbers given to you by your father's best friend's half cousin actually works. Yes, the guy at the other end may actually recognize you as the kid he ran into some ten years earlier at a family function you attended in the Hamptons and, for some reason, he has decided to be magnanimous and invite you to his office. You're going to talk Hollywood. Now, he can't help you—no one ever can—but he is going to give you a list of people to call for the very same reason you approached him.

What People Are Saying Is Not What They Really Mean

Another skill you must learn is the ability to understand what is being said to you. Some might call this reading between the lines, but that would be too kind. I call it this: "Why don't you tell me what you really mean, you obnoxious, paranoid prick whose over-riding desire is to play it safe and keep your job, but just in case you have made an error in judgment you are going to play it safe and give me some useless advice about shopping my film around to others even though you are really in a position to buy it."

OK, time to sharpen your skills. Here are some meetings you may have with people in the entertainment industry. The boldface type relates what that individual says to you out loud, and the italics is what they really mean.

You have been shopping your film around, and you finally get an appointment with a film distributor. After he views the film he makes this statement.

THE TALK: You really should shop your film around to a distributor and see if anybody will pick it up for distribution.

THE TRUTH: This is really one of my favorite types of meetings because I know this person is a distributor, and he knows he is a distributor, so why doesn't he just say, "Sorry, but the film is not what we are looking for." Or even better, why can't he give an honest appraisal of the film? I think we would all appreciate this much more than this charade that XYZ Film Distributor is not really in the film distribution business.

You are meeting with various production companies in the hope one will hire you to direct a film.

THE TALK: You are obviously very talented, but right now things are slow, and we optioned a project last week, so we are going to be busy with that.

THE TRUTH: This is a nice way of saying we are totally uninterested in you and your project. The best way to brush somebody off is to tell them they are talented.

Whatever It Takes

You have to understand that the deck is stacked against anybody trying to make an independent feature film. As an aspiring film-maker, you have to be willing to go that extra step to make your film a reality. Oftentimes this means recognizing a situation and taking advantage of it. Here is how a friend of mine—I'll call him Karl—turned his feature film dreams into reality.

I was working on a low-budget feature called *A Million Miles*. It was a four-week shoot, Mondays through Fridays (no weekends—unheard of). The shoot days were between ten and twelve hours. (Equally unheard of—those are, of course, short days in the independent film circuit.) This gave the cast and crew much free time. This would be my way of making a film, because I certainly wasn't going to pay for everything myself.

A friend of mine had given me seven rolls of recans, because he was moving to England, so I had enough film stock to get started. By becoming friends with the second AC, short ends of film stock "disappeared" out of the camera truck, so now I had even more film.

The first and second ACs acted as DPs on the horror film I would now shoot in secret (they also provided a simple sixteen millimeter package, also from the camera truck). I was the sound man on the "real" film, and the gaffer gave me the keys to his lighting truck after I bribed him with three six-packs of beer (I needed to keep one for myself). This gave us the equipment we needed to shoot and—thanks to the production department for the shooting locations—the motel rooms we were staying in.

During the days of the "real" shoot, I would fill up my

sound cases with snacks from the kraft services table, and take about half of any leftovers from all meals. I would leave a little so no one would get suspicious. This provided us with meals during the four hour shoots on my film.

After a couple of days, the buzz on the "real" film's set about my horror movie, *Mayhem Motel*, was growing. The director was getting wind of something being up, so he came up to me to question things. He would not at all have been into me taking his actors, film stock, food, and everything else for my own. When he asked me if anything was up, I lucked out. Being the soundman, I happened to have my headphones on, so I pretended to get a distress call from my boom operator in the room we were shooting in across the hall. I told the director to hold on, and I ran out of the room we were in. I managed to avoid him for two more days that way.

So anyway, back to the night schedule. In general, things were going well shooting two or three scenes a night (one take per shot, of course—I'm not made out of money). More small problems did arise, however. The people on the "real" film got even more suspicious at times—like when I blew the circuits to half of the motel (don't use too many lights when sneaking around), and when the producer of the "real" film was confronted by the motel management about why there was blood all over the sheets in my room. I told her I reopened a bad cut on my foot and had to limp around for a while. The truth of the matter was, of course, a great stabbing scene shot the night before. Much Karo syrup.

So the down-and-dirty shooting was completed, and I was trying to figure out a way to add my film to the "real" shoot's lab order, but it wasn't going to work. I had to pay for that myself. I guess I can't have everything.

The director finally figured out on the last day (of

both features) what was up. He wasn't too ticked off—his film went OK.

We all had fun, two features were completed, and no one got hurt.

A Million Miles and *Mayhem Motel* are still seeking distribution.

This is an example of recognizing a situation and turning it into a feature-film opportunity. These opportunities appear in different ways, so you have to understand the implications quickly. For example, say your boss has asked you to look after his beach cottage for a month. After accepting this responsibility, the next question you have to ask yourself is this: How fast can I write a script to take advantage of this location?

About a month ago, I was on my way to drop off a reel at an advertising agency. As I shuffled through the radio presets in my car, I stopped on one station long enough to hear a story about a group of American Airlines pilots who decided to run an American flag from Boston to Los Angeles in memory of those aboard the two airplanes that destroyed the World Trade Center.

I immediately drove home, found a way to contact the organizers of this event, then drove up to Boston to meet them. The next morning, I was on my way across country with a crew of four at 5.5 miles per hour.

Keep your eyes open. You never know when a film opportunity may rear its head. Then it's just a matter of reorganizing your life to accommodate the film's production schedule.

Laminants

Laminants are the badges that people wear around their necks attached to a lanyard. These badges always seem to imply special access to something. Not only that, it kind of makes you feel special when you wear one. With this in mind, let's fire up the laser printer and make up some badges. Maybe you can put your film's title on it and then some descriptive term like *crew* or *top team*. I would go with top team; it sounds like you are in charge, and you might be able to cut some lines somewhere because you are wearing it.

Should I Go to Film School?

In general, college is a great time. Late nights of partying and pseudointellectual discussions about the ozone layer and the merits of our system of government. First, let's dispel the biggest myth about college. No, if your roommate dies you will not get a 4.0 grade point average for that semester. So stop draining the brake fluid out of his car, because it will not work.

There are two types of film schools out there: the big and the small. The big ones have close ties to Hollywood and the motion-picture industry. These include the University of Southern California, the University of California, Los Angeles, and New York University. NYU says that it's different; it tries to stress that it is an art school with no industry ties. Don't believe it. NYU is just as wound up in the name game as the other two colleges. When you graduate from any of these schools, you will stand a pretty good chance of landing a job serving coffee to a celebrity. These schools have connections. Their students go out into the world and are proud to help a classmate from their old school.

Then there are all the rest, the smaller film schools. There are many of these schools scattered throughout the country. Of course, we are only talking about schools that have some type of program in production. To do this, they must have film equipment. These schools might have one faculty member who, for a short time, went to Hollywood to make his dream of a feature-film career a reality. Chances are he failed, and now he has resorted to teaching.

All film teachers have a big fish story, the big one that got away. These teachers have big egos based on noncareers in an industry they are supposedly helping you break into. The truth is that they are so bitter and egocentric that they get extreme pleasure every time they drive past the local Photo-mat and see ex-students of theirs selling flash bars and double print sets.

Sure, an occasional PA job might be steered your way, but you won't get paid. It will happen like this. Some production manager who was the teacher's pet some years earlier will hire you for nothing. He will con you into believing that the experience will be a chance of a lifetime. He will tell you that when he was in school, he would traverse rivers, swing from the trees, and climb the highest peaks for this privilege. The truth is you will get coffee, rake leaves, and kiss ass for free.

If you want to be a PA, you might as well skip college and get a jump on the competition. There is no reason you can't take coffee orders right out of high school. You don't need a college education to drive a cube truck and make up fake receipts.

But if you want to write screenplays and get your hands on film equipment and actually make films and learn by going through the process yourself, then film school may be for you.

What About the Student Film?

There is no market for a ten-minute student film. If you make a student film, what are you going to do with it? You are going to enter it into the student academy awards. Then, for two months, you will dream about winning this award, going to Hollywood, and becoming the next directing wonder. But you're not going to win, because in order to win you have to be extremely lucky. Talent is not a factor here.

What about the other contests? Sure, you might win the Oshkosh Film Festival, but what is that going to do for you? *Nothing*. Nobody is going to give you money to make your first feature; you will still be a nobody.

Will I Ever Grow Up?

I can't answer this one.

Getting a Job

In order to get a job, you have to get on the phone. Don't believe that crap when somebody tells you she moved to LA with just one contact, a long-lost relative of a college roommate's cousin. She called this a contact and the next thing she knew she was a PA on the set of a $30 million motion picture. Well, the director got hypothermia, and as she zipped him into a down sleeping bag, he turned to her and said, "Kid? Finish the picture and feel free to drive my Mercedes and live in my Bel-Air estate."

The truth is more like this.

I came to LA with ten contacts and called them all. Half were the wrong number, two were unemployed, and the final three hadn't been connected with the film industry for years.

Call everybody and anybody and be persistent. After a thou-

 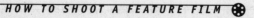

sand calls, you may land yourself a job. And remember, there is always telemarketing.

Also, don't be afraid to work for nothing in order to gain valuable experience on a film set. Do whatever it takes to be on a film set. If you prove your worth, I guarantee someone will start to pay you. The other thing to keep in mind is that film crews often move from one project to another as a unit. So when the crew you volunteered to work for moves on to the next project, and Jimmy the PA has gone home to see his mother, who do you think will take his place? That's right, the superenthusiastic PA who can do anything, and that person is going to be *you*.

Cocky

Filmmakers should be cocky, exuding confidence from every orifice of their bodies. People like that. They want to know that you are capable of taking charge of a multimillion-dollar project. So if you have to be one thing, make it cocky. And remember that cocky is very close to asshole, so be careful not to cross over that line.

Looking Like a Filmmaker

To be a filmmaker, you have to live the lifestyle and look the part. And that requires proper dressing. Go to your closet and gather together all your colored clothing. Take this pile of clothing to the Salvation Army, and don't forget to get a receipt. This is a tax deduction.

In LA, you must wear black. That's right, you have moved to the desert so you can wear black clothing. You should look like the product of a gene-splicing experiment, a mixture of Buddy Holly and Dr. Strangelove. To this look, you must bring your own personality.

Appearance is very important. You will be judged on your wardrobe. Most reps and agents know that anybody incapable of dressing him- or herself in black can't possibly direct. You might also want to consider getting your ear pierced. Left lobe, please—unless you want to send a different message. A tattoo might also be a good choice if you want to portray yourself as a dangerous filmmaker.

How to Take a Publicity Picture

A lot more is riding on this than you think. Remember, in this business, image is everything; yours must be carefully crafted to convey the right message and to set up your career for the path you wish to follow. Get some black-and-white film and load up your camera. Remember to try and convey the proper attitude as you pose for these pictures. Remember, image is everything, so take this seriously. You have to be able to get at least one usable shot out of thirty-six exposures, so don't stress out.

Burning Bridges
and Other Acts of
Vandalism

In the world of film, the idea is to accumulate as many friends and contacts as possible. When you burn someone's lawn because you don't like that person, you are not winning friends. People will tell you that you should be nice because you will meet the same people on the way down that you met on the way up. Well, screw that. If I don't like somebody, why should I be nice to him? I surely don't want that person to be nice to me. Still . . . he might give you a job one day. OK, I'll be nice.

Let's be honest here. Everybody hates anybody who is more successful than he or she is. It's human nature. You are on the bottom right now, so you should hate everybody.

Give 'em hell.

Backstabbing

People love to talk about other people. It's fun—especially when they are not around. So start practicing.

Brownnosing

The art of ass-kissing is very essential for any working professional in the film business without strong family ties. People in the industry like to hire people they know—for example, their friends.

So if you want to get hired, you have to be everybody's friend. To do this, you must continually call up all your contacts and feign an interest in their lives. It is always advisable to call up and talk about a personal matter before moving to business. Here is how a possible phone call might go.

Backstory: Harry the AC is placing a call to Tom the DP, whom he met at the camera rental house earlier in the week. (Notice I have written conversation in script format so I can beef up this book while also plying my trade.)

INT. BEDROOM — NIGHT

A small, overly tidy room. In one corner, film cases containing camera equipment are stacked to the ceiling. A single bed and a desk. HARRY ANDERSON sits at the desk, phone in hand.

> HARRY
> Tom, I wanted to congratulate your
> cine cymbal.

> TOM
> (filtered over the phone)
> Thanks, Harry. How is everything
> going with you?

> HARRY
> Couldn't be better—keeping busy.
> So those cine cymbals must really
> be moving.

> TOM
> I can't complain.

HARRY

Say, Tom, it would really be a
privilege to work on a shoot with
you someday.

TOM

Well, Harry, I do have something
coming on the twenty-fourth.

Harry quickly scratches himself a note.

ON NOTE
Tom possible shoot on twenty-fourth.

HARRY

Well, keep me in mind.

TOM

I will, Harry.

Harry hangs up the phone and dials the next number
on his contact sheet.

Notice how Harry started the conversation by talking about
the other guy and his great accomplishment in developing the cine
cymbal. Harry also made a note of the potential job on the twenty-
fourth. This is to remind himself to call Tom back on the eight-
eenth and ask him about the job again. At the end of the
conversation, Harry moved onto his next contact. Harry is persistent and will call at least five people every night. This is your competition; there are a lot of Harrys out there, so get ready to
brownnose with the best of them.

The Other Guy

Every four to six months, you are going to get really annoyed. This is one of the facts of life. It might happen on a Sunday morning as you innocently leaf through your Sunday paper, or it could be at the end of a newscast or in a magazine you pick up in some waiting room. Regardless, you'll know it when you see it.

It will usually begin with a picture of a young man about twenty-four years old. He will defiantly be wearing a baseball cap, his face captured in either an enormous smile or a very serious look. The serious look means he is pondering the meaning of black holes and if they are connected to Hostess dessert cakes in any way. He will be a filmmaker, that is for sure. He will have signed a contract to direct a feature for a major studio. And here is the clincher: The kid will always say, "When I came to Hollywood, I only had one contact."

The article will never read "I knocked on a thousand doors and finally after ten years of searching I got a call back." No, it will say that he knocked on one door, it popped open, and within three seconds he had a multipicture deal to direct and the option to market his own sportswear.

Take these notices in stride and don't let them ruin your day, because yours will come soon enough.

We Will Make a Million

This is one of the movie fantasies that you may be living. It goes hand in hand with the beautiful starlet beating down your door, shedding her clothes to get the part as the wolf lady in your next film. Neither of these stand very much chance of happening. But by all means, keep the dream alive, because this is as good a reason as any other to get into the movie business.

But look at the reality of film economics. You are going to be eating tuna and macaroni for the rest of your life. The truth hurts, doesn't it? And it doesn't taste so good, either.

Film Books

There is a plethora of books on film. Books on how to make them, how to write them, how to watch them, how to work on one. Go to your local bookstore and leaf through a couple of these books. That's right! They're all the same. They all say the same thing in different ways. Do you really need all these books? No, because I will encapsulate each type of film book into an easy-to-read paragraph, thereby protecting our most precious natural resource—the rain forests—and saving you a hundred or so dollars.

The Screenwriting Book

This book is geared toward the aspiring screenwriter. It will tell you that the only way to learn your craft is to go to the movies and write. Sprinkled throughout this book will be words of encouragement to keep you motivated. There will be a chapter on getting an agent. It will say that you should network, tell everybody you're a writer, and write a really good screenplay. Duh! The last chapter will be a success story, something for you to aspire toward.

The How-To Book

This book will take you through the filmmaking process, kind of like this book. It will tell you that you will need lots of money to make a film. It will tell you of all the legal yet improbable ways of obtaining cash. Various chapters will cover everything from directing to editing. It will have examples of highly profitable films made by cashiers who worked at fast-food establishments in Detroit.

The Inside Hollywood Book

This book is written by somebody who can no longer make a living in the film industry. It will detail the lifestyle of Hollywood, the great parties, sex, drugs, money, and power. Real jerk-off material for those aspiring to make it big. A sprinkling of gossip and name-calling, a dab of funny little anecdotes and a smattering of stories about the author's accomplishments in Hollywood.

Free Magazines

Yup, you heard me right. There are tons and tons of magazines written specifically for the film and video industry, and by this time you have probably spent enough hours in the lobbies or lounges of countless facilities to have leafed through a few of them. Well, they are free. Somewhere inside each magazine is a free subscription card. In return for the magazine, all the publisher asks is for you to tell a few lies about the size of your company, your annual budget for procuring equipment, and other similar questions designed to beef up their database in order to generate more ad revenue. So as you move about, collect these cards and fill them out. Pretend that you are a big company and employ hundreds of people. While you're at it, in this little fantasy world you might spend upwards of a million dollars a year on equipment. The sky is the limit on this little card, so go ahead and dream a little.

The Critic's Book

The books in this genre take movies and analyze them down to the last frame. Usually written by film critics, they will go off on tangents that should leave even the biggest movie buff lost somewhere between Earth and Pluto.

This Book

A loosely assembled piece of trash written from the perspective of a moron trying to break into the film industry.

Rules to Live By in Order to Retain One's Sanity While Trying to Break Into the Film Business

Rule Number 1: Shoot It Yourself, I Don't Do Weddings

As soon as news of your filmmaking venture spreads to your immediate family, the offers are going to start pouring in. Everybody is immediately going to try to hire you, for free, to shoot their wedding on videotape. Don't do it. Shooting a wedding sucks. You have to place yourself in all kinds of embarrassing positions to get the proper shots, you can't drink, and you will be constantly worrying that you didn't get the right shot. Suggest to your tightwad relative who didn't give you one goddamn cent to make your film that he should go out and hire that moron who sells film at the local camera store; after all, chances are he was a recent graduate from the film program at the local community college. Go to the wedding and enjoy yourself. This will be the best food you have eaten in months.

Rule Number 2: What If Somebody Asks What You Do?

You are most likely to encounter this question when you return to that quaint little town where you grew up. You will go to the local tavern to escape from everything that is going wrong in your life and *bingo!* Somebody from that one-room schoolhouse that you grew up in will recognize you. It gets worse. That person will approach and ask you what you are up to. My first move would be to try and bum a drink; at least make this exchange a profitable one. From there, you could try any of the following explanations.

1. Tell him that you're a CPA at a very prestigious accounting firm of Young and Young. This is a blatant lie, but it is absolutely guaranteed that he won't ask you what you do there.

2. You could tell him that you have just finished your first feature film. This will really get him stirred up, and he'll begin to prod into your business. He will ask, "What is it about?" At this point, it would be advisable to duck out of the bar, because the next question will be "What was your budget?"

3. Tell him that you have a house, a wife, three kids, and a dog named Rex. I like this Capraesque answer the best; the possibilities are endless.

Artist

I think this word *Artist* is the most overused word in the English dictionary. Every flake dressed up in black and out of work calls himself an artist. I am tired of hearing it. Everybody claims to be an artist. Businessmen are calling their deals art. Strip miners say they are making art. Enough. I would like to propose the following amendment to the definition of artist to Merriam Webster: A person can only be declared an artist after they have died. That should put an end to all these people running around claiming to be artists.

Under No Circumstances Should You Ever Show Your Mother Your Film

This will result in the standard "What are you doing with yourself" speech. So unless you are making enough money off your films that you don't have to resort to writing stupid film books, you are not allowed to show your mother any movies.

Suicide

If you're going to do it, by all means take a camera with you and film it. Or do it in such a way that your friend can sell the story as a television movie of the week.

Now What Do I Do?

Don't sit around waiting for your phone to ring. Nobody knows who you are, and even if someone does, you will have to call that person. Take your movie around and show it to everybody you know. Keep your fingers crossed, burn some incense, and pray to Buddha—maybe you will make it big.

I Went Respectable and Got Screwed

After making two feature films and squandering all my money and alienating all my friends and tasting cat food, I got a job. A real job in a small production company. My unofficial title was slave boy. I would do everything from changing lightbulbs to buying special inks for the director. In six months, I worked my way up to shooting film. I was a DP, and getting paid for it. I knew I wouldn't work for this makeup-wearing director, who seemed to suffer from

Tourette's syndrome forever. But after a year and three months, after shooting ten commercials, I was summoned to his plywood-infested office. I was told that I would no longer shoot jobs for that company. My mind reeled; just a few day earlier I had walked in on the director in his office clad in nothing but a pair of white BDO briefs listening to clown music. Did I know too much? Was this his way of silencing me? I'll never know because by the end of the week I was fired, gone, out on the street. My brush with going respectable was over. It took me all of two days to get offered a no-budget film, and at the risk of losing my girlfriend I accepted. Please stay tuned.

Tech Support

Sometime during your filmmaking odyssey you are going to have a question. Now, because you bought this book, here is your chance to get the answers in a semitimely fashion. You can send an e-mail to Howtoshoot@hotmail.com, and I will, to the best of my ability, answer your filmmaking questions. And yes, if you are just leafing through the book at the store, I will still answer your question too.

Send Me Your Stories, Tips, and Scams

That's right. If you have a scheme, send it to me and I'll publish it in the next edition of this book.

Never Give Up

I have made numerous films to date with varying degrees of success. Am I where I want to be? No. But one thing I do know is that with every frame of film I shoot I learn a little more about my craft. The rule I live by is this: If I start a project, I am going to finish it. Sure, I might get a bad feeling in the middle, but that is the way the process works. Remember that there is no substitute for going through the process completely and taking your film to the end. So promise me this: Once you decide to embark on a feature-film project, you will finish it. And if it makes you feel any better, I'll tell you this: Right now I have a film hidden in my closet that I will not show anybody. But I finished it, and that's what really counts.

Index

About the Author

Bret Stern started making feature films the day after college. He and some fanatical friends waited for the campus to empty out over Christmas break, and after taking the stuff in the school's equipment room, Bret and his crew spent seven days cranking out a feature film—the only setbacks were the foreign students who raided the set for reading materials and the fake blood with chicken giblets that backed up the dorm's drainage system. After that there was only one alternative left—to keep making movies. A brief stint as a location scout and then as Slaveboy at a New York commercial production company followed. Before getting fired Bret moved up from Slaveboy to Whipping Boy and then shot some commercials as Director of Photography. Once the hammer dropped, Bret had to decide which path to pursue, and although commercial work pays better, who could resist the opportunity to sleep in a cot in a bar for a week and take showers with a garden hose in the basement? What followed were the feature films *Perfect Lies* and *Dark Tides* (where Bret got to sleep on a real bed but he had to share it with his Assistant Director). After much abuse, he fell back into his role as DP, shooting and directing many commercials. Days after he had enough money for the down payment on a house (and faster than his wife could say "Hutch and China set"), Bret was at work on *Road to Park City*, which opened the 2000 Slamdance Film Festival and played in over fifteen others. What's next for Bret? After acquiring the grandfather clock for the house, it was time for the next feature—a sci-fi extravaganza with a budget of $10,000, minus one cent.